Sam Bloom

Sam Bloom

Heartache & Birdsong

Samantha Bloom, Cameron Bloom &
Bradley Trevor Greive

To contact Sam Bloom, regarding corporate speaking engagements, and to contact Cameron Bloom in regards to purchasing art prints of the images featured in this book, as well other official photographs of Sam Bloom and Penguin the Magpie, please go to www.penguinthemagpie.com.

 The ABC 'Wave' device is a trademark of the Australian Broadcasting Corporation and is used under licence by HarperCollinsPublishers Australia

First published in Australia in 2020
by HarperCollins*Publishers* Australia Pty Limited
ABN 36 009 913 517
harpercollins.com.au

HarperCollins*Publishers*
Level 13, 201 Elizabeth Street, Sydney NSW 2000, Australia
Unit D1, 63 Apollo Drive, Rosedale, Auckland 0632, New Zealand
A 53, Sector 57, Noida, UP, India
1 London Bridge Street, London, SE1 9GF, United Kingdom
Bay Adelaide Centre, East Tower, 22 Adelaide Street West,
    41st floor, Toronto, Ontario M5H 4E3, Canada
195 Broadway, New York NY 10007, USA

A catalogue record for this book is available from the National Library of Australia

ISBN 978 0 7333 3979 0

Cover design by HarperCollins Design Studio
Cover and internal photography by Cameron Bloom
Internal design and typesetting by Jane Waterhouse
Photo on pages 184–5: Sam Ruttyn/Newspix
Photo on page 187: Chris Grant/ISA
Colour reproduction by Splitting Image
Printed and bound in China by 1010 Printing

6 5 4 3 2 1   20 21 22 23

For my husband and
our three beautiful sons

Self-pity

I never saw a wild thing

sorry for itself.

A small bird will drop frozen dead from a bough

without ever having felt sorry for itself.

D.H. Lawrence (1929)

Preface

Life is difficult sometimes, and so is the telling of it.

But I want to tell you everything.

To speak aloud the horror, the anger, the pain, the secret shame, the undying love and the desperate hope that made me who I am today.

Though what happened to me is unique, as all transformative experiences are, my story is also the story of every person whose life turned out very differently from their dreams.

I am not the woman I was.

I am not the woman I wanted to be.

I am so much more than that.

Prologue

When I wake up each morning, I die a little bit.

No matter how hard I try not to, I always think about before.
When I was me.

I mourn the life that was taken from me, stolen from my family.
It still seems impossible that it all came to this.

It's easy to be bitter. Easier than breathing.

There's a part of me that's always angry. I don't deny it.

After what I have been through, I now believe there is a darkness inside
all of us. We're all born with it, and if we're lucky most of us will rarely
see it, barely even glimpse it. But if you suffer life-changing loss or
excruciating pain, or both, as I did, it begins to grow. And grow.

The darkness spreads from your thoughts into every nerve and vein of your being until you are consumed by it. Surrender to it, and before you know it you're no longer living your own life, animated only by the darkness. It sculpts deep lines in your face, curls your shoulders forward, hardens the soft places inside you. And no matter how much you fight it, it's always there. You do all you can to beat it back, but you can't rid yourself of it. Even in the happiest of times, it sits in the centre of your being, a jagged pitch-black seed ready to take root and flourish at the first angry thought, the first blood-pulse of frustration and hopelessness.

I cannot tell you how I finally won my personal battle with the darkness, because the battle isn't over, and it may never be.
But I can tell you how I keep going, and why.

To be clear, I'm not a motivational guru or a life coach or a psychologist or a counsellor or any kind of feel-good cheerleader. I'm not the inspirational figure many people would like me to be. If that's what you are searching for, then you'd best look elsewhere.

I can't fix you. I can't even fix myself.

I seldom think of the right words to say to make people feel better about whatever they're going through. More often than not, I don't say anything at all.

And I definitely don't look like someone who has all the answers. I don't have what you might call a 'commanding presence'. I'm the last person you notice when you walk into a room. It's always been this way and I don't take it personally. I'm quiet and small, topping out at five feet and a ponytail. 'Petite' is the sophisticated description, but I'm really just a shrimp.

I've so often been told that because I'm a middle child I should be desperate for attention, which makes me laugh because I am not, by nature, an outgoing person. At all. On the contrary, I'm a true wallflower. Maybe not the shyest, at least once I've had a glass of red wine, or when animals are involved, but pretty damn close.

Talking about myself was never easy, which is why I've always had trouble meeting new people. This may explain why, when I was a little girl, my best friend was a duck called Daisy. And of the two of us, Daisy was easily the more self-assured.

But while I may lack both stature and volume, I don't want for courage – the only things that still make me feel somewhat anxious are public speaking and mathematics.

I've faced all my deepest fears and I'm still here.

That must count for something.

Sam Bloom

I grew up in a normal Australian family … at least to the degree that any Australian family can be considered normal.

It might be simple nostalgia – looking back from my forties while stuck in a wheelchair – but I had a truly wonderful childhood. In my mind, I see nothing but sunshine and endless bright-blue Sydney skies.

I honestly can't recall much about going to school – nothing original or meaningful anyway – but I vividly remember playing in our backyard swimming pool, roller-skating, teaching my baby brother how to ride a skateboard, going on bushwalks through the nearby national park, and stuffing our tiny sunburned cheeks with juicy purple mulberries that grew by our back fence every spring.

Then just when I thought my life couldn't possibly get any better, it did. When I was eight, my parents bought the Surfside Pie Shop in Newport, and our family moved to Bilgola Beach. We had all the cake we could eat and were walking distance to the ocean. Surfing soon became a huge part of my life – I went to bed almost every night with sea salt in my eyelashes. It was a child's paradise.

If I close my eyes I see small bare feet running, always running, on grass, down summer-scorched footpaths and across white-gold sand. I focus on that exact moment when the clean dry sand meets the hightide mark, where the chirp-like squeak of each heel-strike becomes a wet-thud-drumming as I race to the water. It's not a soundscape I was conscious of back then. But it is now.

When I say I was a true water baby, I don't mean I was a gifted swimmer or anything like that. I mean that nothing made me happier than to be in the water, paddling my surfboard out into the line-up at any of the beautiful northern Sydney beaches, or sailboarding on nearby Narrabeen Lakes – a vast, sprawling tidal lagoon surrounded by eucalypt forest teeming with wildlife.

I haven't had much luck with therapists myself; most counselling only seems to amplify my horrid feelings, not ease them. But if I was a trauma psychiatrist I'd just tell every patient to go for a splash at a Sydney beach on a warm, sunny day.

There's something powerful yet calming about the ocean. I love the charged silence of the sea once you get past the roar and blast of the breaking waves – suddenly you are in a space with a completely different energy from all that which you left behind. Nothing that troubled you on land has any hold over you any more. External chaos and internal turmoil yield to breeze and swell. You are physically and emotionally weightless. You are free.

I was barely a teenager when I bought my first surfboard from a local surfer on the beach for fifty dollars – almost everything that I had saved working in the family bakery and babysitting in the evenings. The Malibu board – a red-and-yellow aircraft carrier with an enormous green fin – was nearly twice my height, and I would carry it balanced on my head like a traditional West African porter, as I trudged slowly and carefully down the sand.

My surfing buddies from school would run as fast as they could into the shore break, launching their bodies onto their boards mid-air, then skimming across the water till they were slapped in the face by a wall of whitewash. But that wasn't me. I would take my time, gently dipping my board into the water as if baptising a baby, then slowly paddling out. It wasn't because I was the only girl in the group; it was because I was never in a hurry in the ocean. I wanted this feeling to last forever.

It was out in the water where I was always my true self, or at least my best self. Surfing meant more to me than simply decompressing from a bad day at school. It was more important than just being my favourite sport. It was soothing and invigorating, and somehow healing. It gave me time to think; it gave me a chance to empty my crowded mind. Head raised, eyes alert, body relaxed, I was no longer undersized, because we are all utterly insignificant nothings out there in the big blue. The ocean dwarfs every living thing, even whales, so therefore I was at least equal to all humanity. This is where I belonged.

Once I got out behind the break, I would sit up, catch my breath and read the swell. I loved this moment, bobbing like a gull, watching light dance on the water, getting in sync with the sea. I wasn't chasing the biggest waves; I didn't have any need to show off. I was always waiting for the right wave for me. I loved the smaller, smoother waves, like a ripple of glass. When my perfect wave eventually appeared on the horizon, rushing straight toward me from the belly of the Pacific, I'd heave around my red-and-yellow behemoth and start paddling, slowly at first, and then faster and faster, until my hands were clawing through the water with ferocious purpose to reach that exquisite tipping point, just in front of the wave's foaming lip, when the ocean reclaimed control. In one motion, I would jump to my feet as I was dropping down the sheer blue-green face – a split second of zero gravity – and then my fin would bite into the curling base of the crystal wall. I could feel the ocean's limitless energy surging up through my legs and I would make it my own.

How I ache for that sensation today.

There is a time for stillness, and I cherish quiet hours with nature, a good book and, above all, those I love, but on a planet that is spinning at one thousand miles per hour, much of what makes life worth living is velocity, or at least the memory of it. The salt spray in your face, the wind in your hair, your heartbeat quickening. It's why dogs stick their heads out of car windows, and why rollercoasters exist. When you love the ocean as I do, every wave feels as exhilarating as a first kiss.

One aspect of surfing that I especially appreciate now is how forgiving it is. Don't get me wrong, surfing can be a dangerous sport and surfers are injured every day, especially at the highest level. But for most of us, the water is strangely generous, a soft landing that encourages playfulness. Even when I made a silly mistake that resulted in a spectacular face-first wipeout, it was just a momentary setback. I knew that when I was held underwater by a billion gallons of churning foam for what felt like eternity, it was really just a matter of seconds. By the time I resurfaced, my small explosion of white spray had settled, the water smoothed over. All evidence of my undignified impact was erased, my humiliation likewise washed away. I would smile as I paddled out for more.

The ocean has no memory of our pain.

My dad was a baker; he ran his own business and worked hard all his life. He wasn't very tall but he was strong, his hands and fingers toughened by hauling heavy sacks of sugar and flour. He would spend every day on his feet, tirelessly kneading dough and creating delicious pies, cookies and pastries on flour-dusted benches, and then he would stand watch in front of the red-hot ovens for hours at a time. But he loved what he did and his passion came through in everything he said and touched. Dad raised my siblings and me to believe that sunshine was free, but you had to earn the time to enjoy it. Perhaps that's why I've always loved being outdoors.

When I was six, my dad convinced my mum to pull my big sister, Kylie, my little brother, Ashley, and me out of class for three whole months – an entire school term – just so we could drive across Australia. He argued that we kids would be sure to learn plenty along the way, more than we would from school textbooks, but the truth is that he didn't have any reason for embarking on this epic family expedition other than it was something he'd always wanted to do. At the time, it seemed a little crazy, especially to my poor mum – keep in mind this was forty-odd years ago, and camping was not nearly as comfortable as it is today – but I think deep down each of us understood that every now and then we all need an adventure in order to be truly happy.

We travelled north from Sydney, following the east coast all the way up to Far North Queensland, and then we turned west to Darwin, the saltwater crocodile capital of the world, before heading home via Australia's legendary Red Centre, a vast shape-shifting desert of strange creatures and timeless monuments.

I'll never forget being allowed to stand on the front of our four-wheel drive, leaning forward against the steel bull bar as we drove along the seemingly endless beaches of Fraser Island. Travelling deeper and deeper into the Australian wilderness was such an incredible feeling – especially as a child. Suddenly, the world seemed so much bigger.

Having the power to change your view and experience the unknown is not just a choice that sets us apart from battery hens, it's also the easiest way to grow as a human being.

Now, to be clear, I'm not sure I'd strap my three boys to the front of our car and roar off into the Never Never – but the joy of freedom and discovery has never left me. That glorious family road trip inspired my lifelong love of adventure travel. I was still in pigtails when I set myself the goal of travelling through Africa, a land of ancient cultures and untamed majesty, not unlike our own. But I wouldn't stop there. I wanted to see as much of the world as I possibly could and, if I was lucky enough to have my own family one day, I hoped my children would grow up to finish the job.

Another enduring gift I received from my dad was his outsized love of animals. Thanks to his infectious delight when interacting with creatures of all shapes and sizes, and his hilariously limited appreciation of domestic consequences, there was a never-ending stream of strays and injured wildlife for us to look after: waterfowl, galahs, rabbits, echidnas, kangaroos and, of course, dogs. Keeping the ever-growing menagerie out of the house was a constant battle. Mum was a great sport about it, but her patience was tested when a beefy hare dug up the lawn, and wild ducks started pooing in the pool and savagely pecking any child wearing a swimsuit.

Apart from my loyal duck, Daisy, who was never late for our private picnics and tea parties in the backyard, my favourite member of our ever-expanding family was our Dalmatian, Sally, who was as sweet as honeysuckle and as dumb as a rock cake. She was so gentle and loving, she made me re-evaluate my awe and envy of people who are far smarter than I am. I'll take kindness over genius any day of the week.

Sally was hit by a car on my thirteenth birthday, just after we'd eaten the panda-shaped birthday cake Dad had made – not something a freshly forged teenager is ever likely to forget. I was very upset, we all were. Fortunately, Sally survived the accident, but she suffered serious nerve damage in her right shoulder, which left her lame in her right foreleg. She would drag her foot as she walked or ran, resulting in terrible abrasions and weeping sores. While none of this seemed to bother Sally, we knew we had to do something to prevent a nasty infection, so, after dressing her wounds, we would bundle her paw up in old socks, re-sleeving the paw again and again until it resembled a cuddly grapefruit, so that she could bound around the place without injuring her paw even more. But Sally's treatment didn't stop there.

One of my defining moments as a young girl was watching Mum lifting Sally into the pool and then getting into the water beside her and massaging and manipulating Sally's shoulder and foreleg. Mum undertook this task time and time again – she never made a fuss or even talked about it, she just did it. To be honest, I don't recall it making any difference to Sally's leg; she was lame till the day she died. But Mum didn't care; she wasn't motivated by outcomes, she was motivated by need, so she simply refused to give up on Sally.

Needless to say, my mum's unassuming example made a huge impression on me. And it's clear to me now that, at my best, I inherited my love of life and sense of adventure from my dad, and my quiet strength and compassion from my mum.

The reason I'm telling you all this is that, when you know how my parents inspired me, you'll understand why I wanted to grow up to be nothing less than a 'nurse explorer' – as hilarious as that sounds. I imagined myself travelling to isolated villages in far-off lands, caring for the sick and seeking out lost wonders. In fact, when I was in first grade, my teacher asked each member of our class to draw a picture of what we wanted to be when we finished school, and I drew this: a brave little nurse about to enter the ancient pyramids of Egypt.

What makes me laugh the hardest at this drawing is how big that syringe is, because I hated getting injections as a little girl and I don't like them any more now – I never liked giving them either.

Now I might be small, but I am a determined person by nature and, by the time I met Cam and fell in love, my heart was set on becoming a nurse, and I had resolved to travel to Europe, Asia and, most especially, West Africa.

Sam

'Falling in love' is such a beautiful expression, but in my experience it doesn't really describe the sensation properly. 'Leaping into love' feels closer to the mark.

I adored Cameron from the minute I saw him. He was both shy and ludicrously overconfident, handsome and scruffy, funny, often quite silly and truly spontaneous, and yet very serious about his vocation and tirelessly hardworking. Cam was taller than me, though few people aren't, so that really doesn't mean much. He had a tanned and chiselled surfer body with strong shoulders and incredible abs, but he was an artist, not an athlete. Photography was both his profession and his passion, and Cam's bright-blue eyes were always seeking ways to frame the beauty around him, his camera poised to capture every exquisite composition found in nature.

I was in the second year of my Bachelor of Nursing degree, at the University of Technology, in Sydney, when Cam and I first met. On weekends and during semester breaks, I would work behind the counter for my mum and dad to earn a little extra money. Cam would come into the bakery in the early evening, dripping seawater from his post-work surfing session, and order a hot pie or a sausage roll and a vanilla slice. We would flirt a little, just shy smiles at first, then I'd say hello and toss a treat to his loyal dog – a chunky Staffie with a permanent grin and a bottomless stomach. Eventually, over a few weeks, our flirtation escalated from awkward pleasantries to playful banter to drawn-out conversations about anything and everything and nothing much at all. I had such fun getting to know this delicious man that I would completely lose track of time and whatever I was supposed to be doing. God only knows how many bakery customers we lost because of my besotted daze. And then, just when I wanted to kiss him, Cam would stupidly bumble off home wearing the exact same goofy smile on his face as his dog, trailing wet sand out the door and down the street. The bakery would dim a little when he left, and my heart would reluctantly return to normal size and cadence.

Cam was at the bakery so often that I just assumed he ate dinner there every single day, but then Dad told me he only turned up when I was working. My old man didn't miss a trick. I looked forward to our conversations each afternoon, a lot more than I ever let on, and I'd be quite devastated if for some reason Cam didn't show up. I kept waiting for him to ask me out on a date, but, despite the evident mutual attraction and countless opportunities, he never quite managed to get to the point we were both dancing around. Cam was so shy about his romantic intentions that I began to wonder if this gorgeous idiot was going to mess this up for both of us. Finally I put it all on the line and flat-out told him to invite me to a party taking place at the Newport Arms, a beer garden just down the road. Well, thank goodness I did.

I've loved Cam every day since. We've had a million ups and a few epic downs, but we also have three beautiful sons and have shared more adventures than we can count. I couldn't imagine him not being at the centre of my little world, and I know I could not have survived my accident without his love and support. He truly is both the love of my life and my greatest hero.

Needless to say, once we started dating, I never again complained to my parents about having to work at the family bakery during my university holidays.

Part of what made me confident that Cam was the one for me was that he fully embraced my desire to help people in need and to explore as many countries as possible. Following my graduation, Cam and I bought two oversized backpacks and two return tickets to Rome, and off we went, hand in hand.

The Eternal City was everything I'd imagined and so much more. We ate, we laughed, we explored every narrow cobblestone street, studied every historic monument, and then we ate some more. It was a pre-honeymoon, of sorts. When we could not consume any more handmade pasta without rupturing some vital organ, we departed Italy for Greece, and then continued westward to Turkey, where we celebrated my twenty-second birthday at Trabzon, on the Black Sea.

We had our share of close calls and bad luck. In eastern Turkey, on a train journey from Doğubayazıt, near Mount Ararat, seven local thugs surrounded us inside our carriage and the biggest member of the gang pulled out a knife and brandished it in front of us. Cam and I were sure we were about to be robbed, or worse, but then a young Kurdish apricot farmer, still in his late teens, pushed forward to face them down, pulling out a knife of his own. Amazingly, the would-be train muggers backed down. The apricot farmer invited us to sit with him, on sacks filled with dried apricots, where we'd be safer in his protection. He even cut open the corner of one bulging sack, with the same small but heroic blade, and shared the sweet fruit with us.

In southern Jordan we wanted to camp in Wadi Rum, a crimson desert canyon also known as the Valley of the Moon, made famous by the movie *Lawrence of Arabia*. We had just set up our small tent when a Bedouin goatherder came over to check on us. He quickly and correctly assessed that we were underprepared for our stay and brought us food, water and firewood, politely but adamantly refusing any payment. Then he let us know that his camp was two kilometres up the valley, and that we should call on him and his family at any time if we needed additional assistance.

Everywhere we went, we met wonderful people who made us feel at home, even in the most remote villages. I don't pretend that travel is always safe; it isn't. Self-awareness and common sense are as essential as visas and vaccinations. But innumerable positive encounters have formed an unwavering belief, repeatedly confirmed since my accident, that almost every person you meet is looking for an opportunity to be kind.

The world is simply not as bad as some want us to believe. Regardless of what you see on television or read in the newspaper, I can promise you that no matter where you go, you'll find that people are, by and large, good. The people we met were good in the simplest and truest way; they wanted to share the best of themselves with us, so that our life journeys were that little bit better for having met each other.

We often found that it was those who had the least who were the most generous, and those facing the greatest adversity who were the most concerned about our comfort and safety. So while I certainly loved the postcard views, the intoxicating flavours and aromas, and being woken each morning by birdsong melodies unknown to me, it was the people we met along the way that I treasure most.

By now the travel bug had completely taken over, so instead of returning to Europe we decided to continue south and explore the Middle East. Our collective savings meant that luxury travel was not on the menu. But we were always prepared to rough it in order to see extraordinary places, especially those that were off the beaten path. A feast on paper plates tastes just as good as it does on fine china, and raising a plastic cup of cheap wine does nothing to diminish a heartfelt toast.

We scaled rugged mountains and crossed deserts on horses, on camels, on foot and in decrepit vehicles that seemed held together by sticky tape and prayer. We walked through ancient Syrian cities that have since been reduced to rubble and chaos, such as Aleppo, Palmyra and Damascus. We even stumbled into the middle of a Bedouin wedding in Wadi Musa, on our way back from Jordan's fabled red-stone city of Petra. Neither of us spoke any Arabic, but our exuberant hosts welcomed us warmly, as if two dusty and bewildered Australians were the honoured guests they had long been waiting for. I was hurried away amidst a gaggle of giggling and ululating women and Cam was press-ganged into a raucous throng of menfolk. Both of us enjoyed the wild dancing and singing, and quickly became semi-accustomed to the wanton firing of pistols into the cloudless desert sky. But when the wedding feast was brought out, we both felt the delicious mansaf, paper-thin shrak bread, dates and spiced tea were more than sufficient, and decided to forgo the heaped and pungent platters of boiled camel meat.

We cooled off our dancing feet floating in the Dead Sea while discussing our impromptu pilgrimage of the Holy Land, but when we were denied entry into Israel, due to a recent security alert, we journeyed west instead, into Africa, via Egypt. And that was when, with my very own eyes, I first saw the pyramids I'd drawn as a little girl.

My childhood dream had come true.

It's not enough to simply say we loved adventure travel – we both felt we were born to do this. In our first few years together, we'd covered half the world, and made plans to see the rest. But the realities of life had begun to be felt. We were both running out of money and Cam had photographic assignments piling up back at work. I loved Cam with all my heart, but I also knew I wasn't ready to go home. I needed to see more. I needed to go farther still, even if it meant going alone. And I knew that if Cam felt about me as I did about him, he would wait for me. We didn't argue or fight about it, but this was the first real test of our relationship.

Cam and I tearfully parted ways in London. He returned to Sydney while I stayed on and registered with a local nursing agency, in the hope of finding a short-term job to save enough money to continue my travels in Africa. I was expecting to work on a hospital ward, or perhaps in a retirement village, so I was very surprised to learn I'd been offered a place at a stately Regency home known as The Lawn in Whitchurch, Hampshire, as Lord Alfred Thompson Denning's personal nurse. As I walked up the long driveway and took in the vast and exquisitely manicured grounds, I was a little overawed to say the least. This would prove to be the most extraordinary job I've ever had.

Lord Denning is still regarded by many people, all far more important than me, as England's greatest judge and most influential legal mind and, for better or worse, his entire life was spent near the centre of an endless storm of historic events, including the infamous Profumo affair. But by the time I met him, he was in his mid-nineties and his health was in decline. He had lost his second wife just a year earlier, and the last of his five siblings had been laid to rest not long before that. Despite his genuine physical and emotional pain, Lord Denning was always unfailingly polite and extremely kind to me, as was his entire family.

My working hours were long, but never difficult, as it was a privilege to spend time in Lord Denning's company. I would greet him after breakfast and stay with him till he went to bed at night. When Lord Denning didn't have visitors or charity obligations, he was happiest in his library, where he would burrow in like a bookish wombat for hours on end. Scholarship was his passion throughout his life and I have no doubt that his love of reading sustained him in his golden years.

Lunch was always a rather lavish production that we both looked forward to. As per his literary tastes, Lord Denning was fond of British classics: roast beef with Yorkshire pudding and gravy, followed by spotted dick. After that, we'd both need light exercise to prevent falling into a food coma, so we'd take a slow walk through the grounds, strolling along the River Test, or sometimes we'd just bumble down the seemingly endless driveway to Church Street and back again. Thankfully, dinner was a simpler affair of cold meats, Stilton cheese and Branston pickle, though I still managed to become very chubby in a surprisingly short amount of time.

One of my happiest memories from my time with Lord Denning was joining him and his family for Christmas celebrations at the home of his devoted stepdaughter, Lady Fox, a very distinguished legal mind in her own right. The company was lovely, Lady Fox was incredibly kind, and the food was to die for (roast turkey with sweet prunes in the stuffing – oh my God!), but then it snowed and I was utterly spellbound. The English countryside draped in glittering white looked like something from a children's pantomime or a nineteenth-century greeting card, almost too serene, pretty and perfect to be taken seriously. It was such different beauty from anything I'd seen in Australia, the Middle East and Africa. I felt so very lucky to be wintering in this magical land.

Lord Denning was very interested in the fact that I was going to return to Africa and he interrogated me about my solo travel plans over countless lunches, both concerned and delighted for me in equal measure. When the day came for me to tell him that I'd booked a one-way plane ticket to Senegal, and that I was finally moving on, he gave me an enormous hug and presented me with a signed copy of his family's history, along with a very touching private letter that I treasure to this day. I thoroughly enjoyed my time at The Lawn; it was an honour to care for Lord Denning, and years later I was very sad to hear he had passed away, barely one month after his one-hundredth birthday.

I was made aware of Lord Denning's vast achievements and exalted stature before I met him, but what I saw when I greeted him every morning was simply a person who badly needed my help. Lord Denning had reached a place in his life where thinking about what he had lost occupied him far more than what he had to look forward to. Not that he wasn't often bright and cheerful, because he was, and I don't blame him either way. As I have learned, each of us has our own threshold of pain and loss and, once we have suffered as much as we can bear, rising up to face a new day, let alone to embrace new opportunities, can seem an insurmountable challenge.

The greater lesson I received from Lord Denning, that I only realised quite recently, is that we will all need help at some point in our lives, no matter how brilliant or strong or rich or celebrated or powerful we might be. And when help is forthcoming, and we can accept it graciously, our lives are so much better for it. Lord Denning's humility and gratitude for the help he received is something that I constantly strive to emulate.

My return to Africa was bittersweet. I was thrilled to be living out an adventure I'd looked forward to my whole life, and it easily surpassed all my childhood fantasies, but I also missed Cam. I would undertake several amazing journeys on my own that changed my life – traversing the African continent from west to east, and trekking from Bhutan's Tiger's Nest Monastery to the base of the snow-covered peaks that guard the borderlands. Every journey enriched my life; however, my first solo African trip, when I was twenty-two, made a significant impact on me, one that haunts and inspires me to this day – but I'll come back to this later in my story for reasons that will become clear.

My reunion with Cam was everything. We made a home together in Sydney and I joined the neurosurgical ward of the Royal Prince Alfred Hospital in Camperdown, but it wasn't long before we started saving for plane tickets. By that time, I had already travelled throughout West Africa and beyond, I'd cared for members of noble and wealthy families and also the least fortunate. Nevertheless, there was so much left to see and do and I wanted to experience all of it. As self-sufficient as I was, I had to admit that life seemed more vivid, more exciting, more fun and somehow everything tasted better when Cam was by my side.

The Horn of Africa was a highpoint for us in so many ways. We searched for Ethiopia's elusive red wolves in the Simien Mountains, and joined in the Timqat celebrations in Lalibela, where we followed the Tabot, a sacred replica of the Ark of the Covenant, from a ritual baptism site to its holy resting place, followed by feasting and dancing in a sweet and tangy cloud of exotic incense.

The sensory overload continued wherever we went. On the shores of Lake Turkana, we met a local fisherman cooking at the side of the road, who happily grilled two enormous fleshy white fillets of Nile perch for us that have never been equalled since. In Addis Ababa, we ate a mouth-watering meat-and-vegetable wat using only our fingers, and scrumptious injera bread made from finely ground grass seeds. And to this day, every time we enjoy a really good cup of coffee, we think of the wondrously aromatic coffee ceremony we were privileged to attend, during which each guest drinks three small bowl-like cups of hot, dark nectar. From first to last, mildest to most intense, each cup is given a unique name, with the third and final cup being called 'Baraka'. Put simply if not literally, *baraka* means 'blessing', but more accurately it embodies the rather beautiful beliefs of the Islamic mystics wherein *baraka* represents God's divine blessing passing around, into and through you in the form of his spiritual presence.

Not long after this, I found out I was pregnant, which was the greatest blessing I could ever imagine.

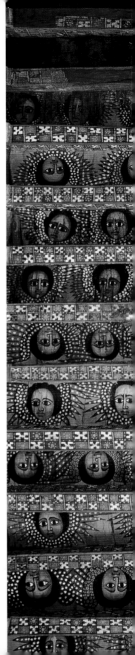

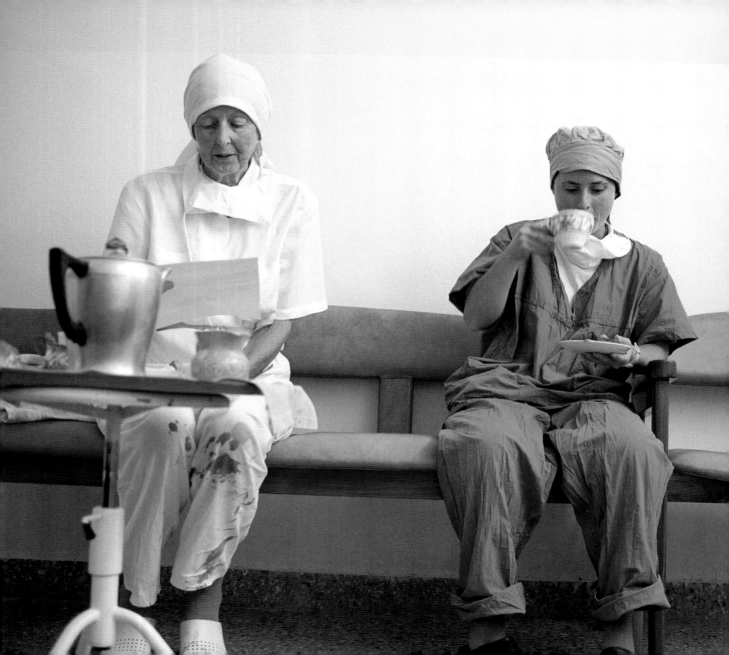

Before we came home, we had the honour of meeting one of my heroes, Dr Catherine Hamlin, at the obstetric fistula hospital she founded with her late husband, Dr Reginald Hamlin, in the Ethiopian capital. For sixty years, Dr Hamlin has dedicated herself to providing free surgical care to women – by which I mean young women, often little more than girls – who have suffered an obstetric fistula. This is where a badly obstructed childbirth has, after two, three or even five days of excruciating labour, resulted in a ruptured birth canal and also, in almost every instance, the death of the woman's precious baby. The primary reason for this tragedy is that girls are still forced into arranged marriages, many of which amount to an especially abusive form of sex slavery, with some girls being as young as eight or nine; they're pregnant long before their tiny bodies are remotely ready to bear children. Tens of thousands of these tweens and teens die in childbirth. Those who survive often wish they'd died as well.

The gaping tear between the birth canal, the urinary tract and the rectum often results in hideous complications, serious infections, constant agony, complete incontinence, and continually leaking foul-smelling discharges of urine and faeces. In some especially horrible cases, the protracted labour places so much pressure on the girl's pelvis that it causes long-term nerve damage. Some women are physically unable to straighten their bodies or walk afterward, and have to resort to crawling on the ground like an animal.

Unable to live a normal life, ruined by shame and discomfort, these girls are humiliated by their damaged bodies and ostracised by their communities. Often deemed disgusting by their husbands, they are abandoned by their own families and forced to leave their homes. Many are destined to live alone in misery and squalor, far away from all they know and love. The World Health Organisation estimates that more than two million young women are currently living with untreated obstetric fistula in Asia and sub-Saharan Africa alone, and that there are one hundred thousand new patients in need of care every year.

Catherine is softly spoken and as humble as a saint, but it was abundantly clear how much she loved Ethiopia and its people, and how incredibly passionate she was about helping the poor girls who would come to see her. Catherine's modest home was on the hospital grounds, surrounded by a bright and beautiful garden of crimson roses and yellow, pink and purple bougainvillea, from which she would cut flowers to place in a white floral vase on the dining table inside the small cottage that she shared with her black Labrador, Chips.

Catherine spoke to us about the legions of forsaken women who would beg at the bus shelters for weeks, months and even years just to save enough to travel from their small towns and remote villages to Ethiopia's capital city to seek treatment. These were journeys of desperation and resilience. When Catherine told Cam and me about one woman who was forced to beg for seven years in order to get the help she badly needed, we couldn't hold back our tears.

I met some of the fortunate girls who had finally made it to the hospital after living through terrible hardship. They were exhausted, relieved, grim, anxious, hopeful, refusing to hope. Some were smiling, some were crying, most hid their emotions; they'd endured so much for so long that it must have seemed impossible that there could ever be an end to their suffering. Even after admission, some patients chose to sit outside the hospital, on the edge of a large gutter, refusing to leave the drain for fear of alienating anyone with their incontinence.

I also met young women Catherine had successfully operated on, and they were transformed within and without. After each patient had recovered, they were given a new dress to wear home, and the pure joy they radiated was all you needed to see to know that their health, dignity and self-respect had been restored.

While most women came and left the hospital alone, a small number of kind and devoted husbands remained with their wives throughout their stay – we met just two during our visit – but the love and happiness they shared was the envy of the world.

Sadly, not every woman was eligible for surgical repair. Some had suffered such terrible damage that it could never be fully undone, and my heart broke for them. But the wonderful thing is that Catherine did all she could to make them whole as well. In addition to providing incontinence pads and ongoing medical care, she gave them a home, an education, and a job at her hospital.

One former patient I'll never forget was a young woman named Mamitu, who had arrived at the hospital when she was just sixteen years old. Her internal injuries were so great that there was no hope of complete surgical repair and a lifetime spent managing her incontinence was all she could look forward to. But Mamitu refused to focus on her own hardship. Instead, she committed herself to making a difference to the lives of others. Catherine told me that Mamitu was a keen observer and quickly took on ever-increasing responsibilities within the hospital. Starting out cleaning rooms and making beds, she moved on to preparing equipment and patients for procedures and, after learning English, became an invaluable medical translator. Under the guidance and tutelage of senior nurses and Catherine's late husband, Mamitu began to assist with surgeries as a theatre nurse and, following countless hours of hands-on theatre experience, she developed into a gifted surgeon without any formal training. Her passion for helping others awakened an incredible gift that, had she stayed in her village, might well have remained dormant her entire life. When I met Mamitu, she had already completed over one thousand successful obstetric fistula surgeries.

Catherine, Reg, Mamitu and their team represented everything I wanted to be when I first decided to become a nurse.

Cam and I hadn't given much thought to family planning. The truth is we'd been caught up in the romance of a moonlit evening while camping in Kenya, and roughly nine months later I was being rushed into a maternity ward at the Royal Hospital for Women in Randwick. I was frightened and excited all at the same time. I had no idea what was to come, which was probably for the best.

After almost twenty-four hours in labour, and what seemed like forever in the delivery room, my natural birth plan got a little wobbly, then fell apart. My unborn son was experiencing dangerous levels of foetal distress, and when it was clear his life was in jeopardy the decision was made to perform an emergency Caesarean. In the midst of this surreal high-stakes medical drama, my spinal epidural had not had nearly enough time to take effect, so when the surgeon's bright scalpel cut through my belly, it felt like I was being eaten alive and involuntary tears streamed down my face. I somehow managed to let the anaesthetist know I was in terrible pain and he dialled up the anaesthetic till I could no longer move my arms or legs, which was extremely unsettling in a different way. I knew I was in shock, but I wanted to see my child take his first breath and know that he was safe, so I hung on with all that I had till I could see his tiny grumpy face. Totally worth it.

I had no idea I would love motherhood so much – I'm certainly not saying I was the world's greatest mum, but it certainly brought out something strong and beautiful in me. I didn't believe childbirth could possibly be any worse the next time, and I'm happy to say I was right. Which is how we ended up with three wonderful baby boys: Rueben, Noah and Oliver.

From the moment I looked into their eyes, I wanted to do everything I could to be a good example to my kids. Just as my dad had taught me, from a very early age I urged them to get outside and enjoy the sunshine – thankfully they didn't need much encouragement. At first, they came to watch their mum play soccer, skate and surf, but in time they joined in. And soon we were doing everything together. Our garage was always filled with muddy sports gear and an ever-growing collection of surfboards. Playing with my three sons and making them laugh made me feel as light and as happy as is humanly possible.

Three months after my dad's funeral, which I'll come back to later, Cam and I decided our three boys, now aged ten, nine and seven, were finally old enough for international travel. We both wanted to pick up where we had left off on our last global expedition, in Botswana and Kenya, but the world had changed so much since then. For the first time in our lives, we chose the safest, closest option available and we departed Sydney, bound for Thailand.

The moment we arrived in Phuket, we knew we couldn't stay there very long; it was too bright, too loud, too busy and too touristy. So we did what we do best – we went searching for the real thing. The next day, we crammed ourselves into a minivan and drove to the South China Sea and then headed north along the coast. We just kept driving, deeper and deeper into rural Thailand, until we spotted a small, no-frills hotel in a tiny village beside an empty stretch of beach. My heart said yes.

On our first morning, there wasn't a cloud in the sky. Cam and I followed our overexcited sons to the beach, where we built a cubby house out of driftwood and coconut palm fronds, and swam in the sparkling waves. Playing with my young family in this authentic slice of paradise was everything I'd hoped for. Beautiful doesn't even begin to describe how it looked and how it felt. The boys were already trying to learn Thai words and phrases, and I knew in my heart my children were going to fall in love with travel and exploration just as my husband and I had years before they were born. I was so proud of them and so excited for them. We all talked over each other about our afternoon plans while sipping freshly squeezed tropical fruit juice – I had absolutely no idea it would be the last thing I would ever taste. Or that this would be my last perfect moment.

If only I could have stopped time.

In that instant, I had the perfect life. I'd become a nurse, a wife and a mother. I'd followed my passion and found true love without losing my independence.

I was the person I was always meant to be.

The person I wish I still was.

I am blessed to have no memory of my accident, but the basic facts are these:

After our morning swim, we all climbed a spiral stairway to the hotel's two-storey observation deck to take in our surroundings and get a better sense of where we were.

Perhaps I was searching for the most promising waves or surveying the surrounding countryside, or maybe I wanted a better look at the hulking water buffalo grazing nearby, I'll never know. But at some point, I leaned against the safety barrier and it failed to do the one thing it was built for.

My husband and my three sons each have a slightly different recollection of what happened next – I'm told traumatic memories are different for every witness – but it doesn't matter, because the result is always the same. The steel railings fell away from the concrete and timber platform and I fell with them – six metres straight down, headfirst onto the blue concrete tiles below, where I lay broken and still in a pool of my own blood.

Apparently, I cried out while paramedics were trying to save my life. I'm told I sobbed out unintelligible words in the ambulance, while my devastated husband crouched by my side.

Rueben, Noah and Oli, the colour shocked from their faces, were squashed into the front seat beside the driver, grimly clutching plastic-wrapped cheese-and-tomato sandwiches forced on them by the distraught hotel manager. They kept looking back to their father through a tiny glass window for words of hope, and when none were spoken they stared down at the soles of their bare feet, stained red by their mother's blood.

The emergency room at the nearest hospital couldn't help us, my injuries were too severe, so we set off again in chaotic stop-and-go traffic – Cam pleading, then shouting at the driver to turn the siren on. The electronic wailing began and we lurched forward, racing to speeds of one hundred and sixty kilometres per hour. No one was wearing seatbelts.

Four agonising hours later, we arrived at the emergency entrance of a second hospital and I was carried into the critical care unit. It didn't look good.

Once I was admitted and receiving treatment, Cam shuttled back and forth between critical care and the lobby, where our three boys were told to wait. Cam tried his best to keep it together for the sake of the children, even though he believed I could die at any minute. He hugged our sons, and wiped away the vomit from the corner of Oli's mouth, before finding a quiet hallway in the hospital to weep in private. Then he started calling family in Australia to come up with a plan to help care for the boys in the event of my death.

But it wasn't my time.

I recall lying beneath a bright light, then an intravenous line was inserted into my left internal jugular vein. The sharp pain in my neck was immediate and I grabbed a white cotton sheet and squeezed it tightly in my fist. A blue-gloved hand raised my blood-soaked t-shirt into my field of vision and another one cut it off me with scissors. An oxygen mask was placed over my mouth.

Days later, when I woke up surrounded by Thai doctors and nurses, I could not even begin to fathom the horrific nature of what had happened. I just knew that every bone, muscle fibre, blood cell, nerve ending and even hair follicle was in terrible pain.

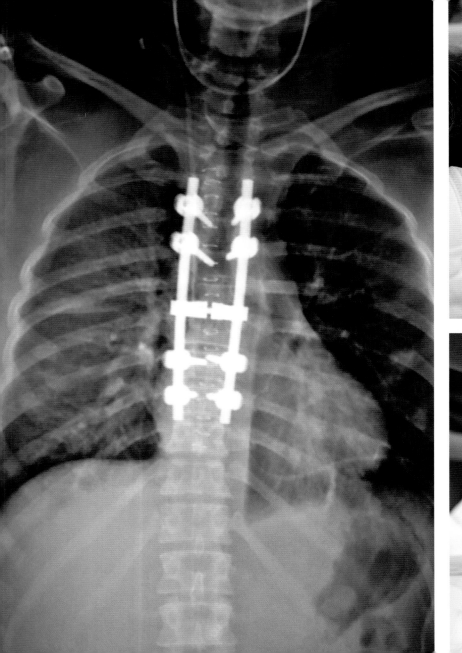
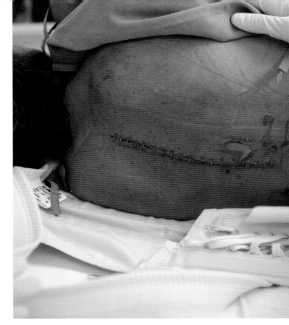
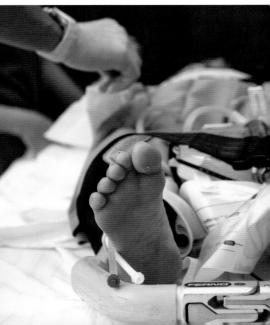

The medical records state that my skull was fractured in several places, and my brain was bruised and bleeding – which explains why my headache was incredible, as if a small bomb had exploded a few centimetres behind my eyes.

It was impossible to think.

I'd lost my sense of taste and smell.

My teeth had been hammered right through my tongue on impact – I have no idea how much blood I had swallowed. My face and jaw felt swollen tight. Just thinking about speaking was excruciating and the physical act of forming sentences was almost impossible. Even breathing was hard.

Both of my lungs had ruptured, and my left lung had completely collapsed due to my chest cavity filling with blood.

There were tubes coming out of my neck, arms and back. I was still strapped to a spinal board. I couldn't sit up. I could barely move a single muscle.

My whole body felt battered, that much was painfully clear to me. But I had no idea a fist-shaped knot of bone had punched out through my back, and that my spine was shattered at T6 and T7 – roughly in line with my chest.

My first lucid memory is of blinding agony raging throughout my head, as if my skull was being crushed and torn apart at the same time. Thanks to my brain injuries, and a heavy dosage of pain medication, I lost all sense of time and place. I drifted in and out of awareness. I saw my husband's grim smile and my ashen-faced little boys, and I knew things looked pretty bad. Or at least I thought I knew. When I tried to speak to my boys, they were gone, and instead my mother had appeared; in the time between closing and opening my eyes, she had flown to Thailand from Australia.

Mum said a hundred reassuring things and asked a hundred questions about how I was feeling, none of which I recall answering. Instead I shouted, 'Mum, the straps are hurting my boobs!' God only knows what she made of that. And then I was lost again, drifting back into my medicated storm of pain and oblivion.

I was not aware of the many hushed conversations about whether I would live or die.

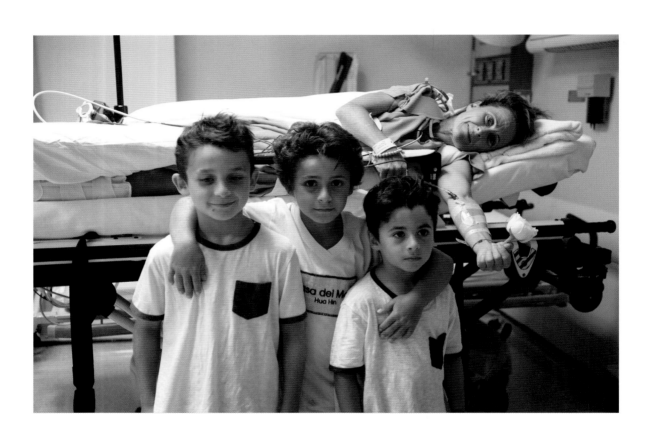

At some point after my lifesaving surgery – hours, days or weeks later, I really have no idea – I found I was able to speak more easily despite the discomfort, and no longer relied on monosyllabic grunts. Cam had stayed by my side throughout and the boys visited me every day. I didn't have a mirror and could only partially explore my swollen and sutured skull and rebuilt torso with my fingers, so I couldn't know what I looked like, but their sad little faces told me everything I needed to know about my condition. They were terrified. The internal bleeding in my scalp had run down both sides of my temples and cheeks, so almost half my face was a revolting blue-purple.

Seeing my family suffer, all because of me, made me feel sick with guilt – I mean, what kind of idiot falls off a balcony? What kind of mother exposes their children to this kind of horror? What kind of wife shatters her body and her family and then leaves her husband to pick up the pieces? I felt terrible for putting them through all this; I wanted them to know how sorry I was for frightening them and for ruining their holiday. I kept telling them that everything was going to be all right and that Mummy was going to be okay, even though I honestly had no idea what the outcome would be.

I hadn't felt any meaningful sensation below my chest since I regained consciousness, and while you'd imagine that I would be freaking out about not being able to feel two-thirds of my body, I really wasn't. Not because I was resigned to my fate, but because I had so much else to deal with – I was in excruciating pain and I was understandably fixated on whether or not I would be permanently brain-damaged, and frankly the mere idea of being paralysed was so utterly horrific that it seemed impossible that this could ever happen to me.

I learned the hard way that being a medical professional counts for almost nothing when you are undergoing intensive care – years of training evaporates as your mind and body rally all their reserves against death.

To complicate things even more, the combination of the language barrier, courteous Thai etiquette and local hospital protocol were such that no one actually told me I could be paralysed. I was led to believe I was suffering from spinal shock, and that once the inflammation had reduced sufficiently, in roughly six weeks or so, normal nervous system function should resume. This was still a little frightening, but I was more or less at peace with this diagnosis.

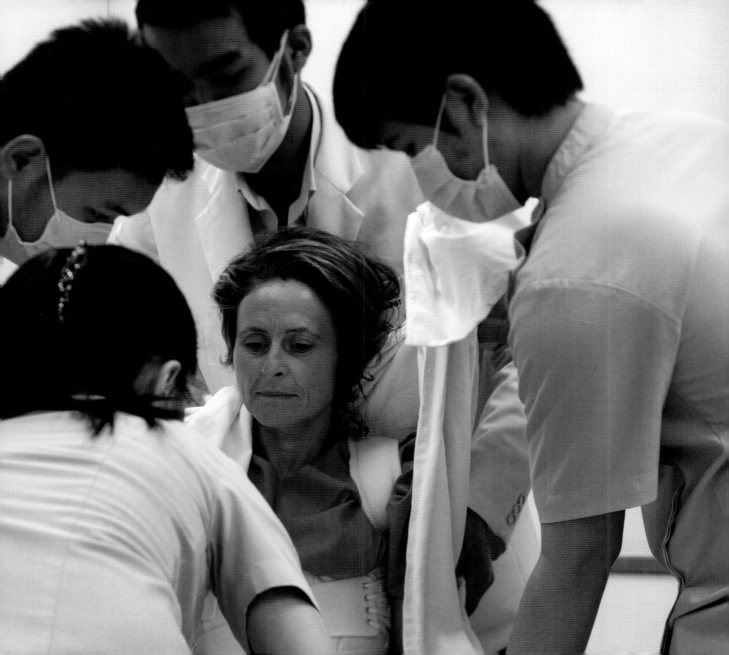

As soon as I could be moved safely, I was flown back to Australia for further treatment, escorted onboard the 747 by an Australian doctor and a Thai nurse. When we touched down at Sydney International Airport, we were galloped through passport control and customs, and then I was transferred onto a stretcher by three hulking Aussie paramedics dressed in dark blue, who were far too professional to laugh at my Thai Airways pyjamas. It wasn't how I'd planned my family holiday homecoming.

My mum and sister were waiting for me at the emergency department of Royal North Shore Hospital, where I was examined by a neurosurgeon who explained my loss of taste and smell would be permanent.

Then I was admitted to the spinal ward, and this is where I learned the awful truth. A young doctor came to see me after reviewing my MRI scans to tell me that, on a scale of moderate to severe, my injuries were definitely severe. When I nervously posed the question of when I might recover sensation in my lower body, the absurdity of it overwhelmed his bedside manner and he openly scoffed at the idea that my spinal cord could ever be repaired to any functional degree. I felt like I had fallen from the observation deck once more.

I would never walk again, I would never stand again, I would never sit up without help. I was no longer an independent woman or a fully capable mother. My surfing days were over. I was disabled, seriously disabled, and nothing more. I burst into tears when I received this news, and, to be honest, I've struggled with this reality ever since.

My mum wanted to punch the young doctor in the face.

Now, if you were hoping to hear how I decided to not let my disability slow me down and was determined to stay upbeat and just get on with my life as if nothing had happened, well, this is probably not the book for you.

The truth is far darker, I'm afraid.

I think the best way to explain how I felt is to tell you how my father died.

Dad didn't just make the best cakes and pies, he also liked to eat them, and he was known to enjoy a cold beer after a long day in front of the ovens. Suffice it to say he'd gotten a little heavier in late-middle age; not what you'd call fat exactly, but as stocky as a pocket gorilla. None of us suspected Dad had any medical concerns until he was diagnosed with type 2 diabetes.

And then he started having heart problems.

All of this, when combined with his physically demanding job at the bakery, was far from ideal.

Mum and us kids would constantly beg Dad to focus on his health, but that wasn't how he was wired. He'd just smile and say, 'No worries, mate. She'll be right.' That was typical Dad. Even after he'd had a heart attack and coronary bypass surgery, he never made a fuss. By then he had terrible circulation in his legs, thanks to cardiovascular disease, and when he injured his big toe he quickly developed an ulcer that was incredibly painful and just wouldn't heal.

He put up with this for a long time. Far too long. He was scarily stoic and wouldn't let it upset him, but he wouldn't take any meaningful action to improve his condition either. Whenever we'd visit as a family, I remember always saying to our rambunctious little boys, 'Be careful, watch out for Poppy's toe!'

I was at the gym when Mum called, asking me to come over because Dad's blood sugar level was through the roof and she needed medical advice. When I arrived, I could see the situation was serious, and the numbers were indeed very bad, but this wasn't my field and I didn't know how much insulin to give him, or even if insulin would be enough to help him at this point, so I drove Dad to Mona Vale Hospital to get help.

It didn't go well.

Dad and I were taken into an examination room and the atmosphere was uneasy at best. It soon got worse. Much worse. An hour later, I called my mum and my sister, asking them to come to the hospital as soon as possible because Dad's diagnosis was grave. The infection in his toe had become aggressive; black necrosis was spreading rapidly and the surgeon informed Dad, in no uncertain terms, that amputating his right leg was now his only hope of survival.

Dad was terrified at the thought of losing his leg, yet his fear made him strangely stubborn. He was adamant that he wouldn't go ahead with it; he didn't want to do it, he didn't need to do it. The doctor didn't give up easily. He shepherded the rest of the family into a tiny consultation room and urged us to convince Dad to change his mind, insisting that this was a critical lifesaving measure. We were all frightened, especially me – I badgered Dad to reconsider, asking him to think of his grandkids. But, in the end, we all respected Dad's decision and hoped for the best. He might have looked cuddly, but we knew he was as tough as rugby boot leather, and if he felt he could beat this, then we wanted to believe him.

The medical team bombarded Dad's system with targeted antibiotics and dosed him up with painkillers. Dad was a bit confused from the medication, but his spirits were as high as ever. We would spend every day with him, talking and laughing – at one point he pretended his catheter tube was a fishing rod and that he'd hooked a monster barramundi. Dad was certain he was going to be all right.

But the battle was already lost. Gangrene had set in and he died a few days later.

Dad was cremated, as per his wishes, and his ashes were to be taken up north and scattered in the World Heritage-listed Daintree Rainforest … but somehow they got no farther than Mum's wardrobe.

Dad could still be with us today, enjoying retirement and making treats for his grandkids, if he'd agreed to sacrifice a limb to save his life. But for such a physical person, the thought of hobbling about on one leg was so horrific to him that he decided he'd rather die than be disabled.

Well, now I know exactly how he felt.

During those first days at Royal North Shore Hospital, knowing now what I was, what I had become, I was filled with overwhelming feelings of anger, horror, remorse, guilt and disgust. I was repulsed by my own body – two-thirds of me was dead; my lifeless belly and legs felt revolting, like clammy uncooked pork, and I refused to touch them. I regretted and resented every single thing I'd ever said or done that had led me to that fateful moment by the safety barrier.

The only thing that kept me sane was the thought of going home. I wanted as much of my old life back as possible and I couldn't get out of hospital quick enough. But pretty much nothing seemed to be going my way.

After my fall, I lost so much blood that my blood pressure was too low to survive emergency surgery on my spine at the Thai hospital. Even after several blood transfusions, I remained too unstable to be operated on, so I was parked in a corner of the intensive care unit and my condition was monitored closely so that I could be wheeled into theatre as soon as my odds of surviving exceeded those of dying.

It took three days and three nights.

During that time, afraid that moving me even slightly might prove fatal, the Thai critical care team had kept me strapped to a rigid spinal board, and this resulted in a grade four pressure sore on my lower back. When I was admitted to Royal North Shore Hospital, the skin was already turning dark and disgusting, just like Dad's gangrenous leg. A puddle of dead tissue at the centre of the ulcer was rotting and the necrosis was spreading. I couldn't feel the pain and I couldn't smell the foul odour of putrid meat and sweetened condensed milk, but the doctors knew that if the necrosis got into my spine I was finished, so they wheeled me back into surgery. The theatre nurse who prepped me in the anaesthetic bay already knew what had happened to me in Thailand, and when she saw the pressure sore she started weeping.

I needed three more operations in the end – two debridement surgeries to suck and scrape the dead flesh from the ulcer in order to remove the infected tissue and encourage healing, and then another to seal the gaping crimson crater with a skin graft, cut from my thigh. My time in hospital was extended to seven months.

The first eight weeks were the hardest. I was forced to lie on my side at all times. I would sleep on my side, I was showered on my side on a special trolley, I would even eat on my side. Not that I had any appetite, but I had already lost twenty per cent of my body weight, and without additional protein my pressure sore would not heal. So I would slowly shovel food that I couldn't taste into my ungrateful mouth, and then I would just lie there staring at the walls. For hours on end, I'd count the horizontal coloured lines on the curtains over and over: white, yellow, orange, dark orange, white, red, light green, white, dark green, mid green, and repeat.

The nurses had to turn me over every two hours, day and night. It took two or sometimes three nurses to do the job properly, a smooth rotation without any twisting or jerking. I didn't make it easy for them – every single time I was mid-turn, I'd panic; my lack of body awareness and post-traumatic fear of falling would cause me to lunge-grab on to the nearest part of the nearest nurse and hold on for dear life. I would apologise profusely for startling them and I'd promise myself I wouldn't do it next time. A promise I would break two hours later.

Visits were both lovely and difficult. I was desperate to be with my friends and loved ones, but also hated them seeing me like this. They did everything they could to cheer me up, sometimes bringing picnics for us to eat outside the ward, in the sunshine. But my self-loathing and self-pity were toxic and pervasive. By the time each visit ended, everybody felt sad.

Once my pressure sore had fully healed, I was taught how to drag myself upright, by propping on my elbows and grabbing the bed rail, so that I could be more independent. Then, to encourage greater mobility, and even further independence, I was shown how to use a slide-board to get out of bed and into a wheelchair. It was a two-person job.

Moving from the spinal ward to the spinal rehabilitation unit was not pleasant. This outdated and depressing facility, which has since been demolished, was run down, filthy and in complete disarray, far worse than anything I'd seen in Africa. For me it was especially jarring, as I had occasionally worked here as a nurse fifteen years earlier, when it housed profoundly disabled patients, many of whom had suffered traumatic brain damage and needed constant care. The negative association in my mind was even less uplifting than the grubby floors, bare walls and decrepit furniture. This is where people went to be forgotten.

On my first day of counselling, the resident psychologist suggested I have a hysterectomy to avoid the mess and inconvenience of future menstrual cycles. I was feeling less human by the minute.

To be fair, the rest of the staff were simply wonderful, but I was bitter and angry and obsessed with my loss of function. I had given up before I'd even started; I had already demanded that Cam give away my mountain bike and surfboards.

I was going nowhere fast and I was in good company. Of the fifteen or twenty spinal cord injury patients I lived with, some had significantly more physical function than I did, but most were far worse off. There weren't many women to talk to; it was almost exclusively young men. Still, while being stuck in a wheelchair didn't make me less of an introvert, at least I could be near people who knew exactly what I was feeling.

During our two mandatory group meals each day, it wasn't uncommon for at least one of us to erupt in anguish and impotent rage, violently wiping plates of food and glasses of water off the table to shatter and splatter on the bleak, porridge-coloured linoleum.

I spoke with a teenager who, like me, had fallen from a balcony and broken his back. He told me he was cleaning windows when the accident happened, but later I learned that he had been trying to kill himself. On the anniversary of his first failed suicide attempt, he tried again, by hanging himself from a doorknob. His brain died, but his body survived, until his parents agreed to let the hospital turn off his life support. Only then was he at peace.

And I'll never forget a super friendly guy in his late twenties who showed me a video taken by his best friend that he'd posted on his Facebook page. It starts with him laughing as he runs up a small sand dune onto a concrete footpath that heads out onto a bridge over the entrance to Narrabeen Lagoon, not far from where I've lived all my life. He reaches the midpoint of the bridge, steps over the low safety barrier and onto a large metal pipe running parallel to the bridge. For a second he stands there, grinning, arms outstretched like a crucifix, mugging to his delighted friends who are expecting a comedic acrobatic leap into the water, just two metres below. But he doesn't leap. He executes an elegant swan dive into clear blue water that was far shallower than anyone would have thought. Thankfully, you can't see his neck snap as his head is smashed back behind his body on impact … but when he floats to the surface, face down, completely still, there is no doubt what has just happened. And then the video footage turns manic as his horrified friends rush into the water to save his life. When I last saw him at the spinal rehab unit, he had just enough strength in his fingers to grip a cigarette.

Enter any room and you felt you'd stumbled in on a funeral, it really was that sad. I went to the gym every day, for hours on end, just to escape my god-awful room. Sometimes I'd put on boxing gloves and try to beat the negative feelings out of my system, but this never worked. So instead I'd usually sit around in the gym with one or two fellow patients and we'd take turns regurgitating our self-loathing. It wasn't much, but it helped.

Even then, when I was completely down on myself, prone to extended bouts of whinging and about as welcoming as a bean bag filled with broken glass, I was still very grateful for the tireless rehab staff – especially the sports and recreation officer, who brought such amazing energy to his job every day. He found out about my athletic background and tirelessly encouraged me to take up new sporting interests. He took me to wheelchair rugby games every week, affectionately known as 'murder ball', which was a thrilling sport to watch. He barraged me with suggestions for new sports I might enjoy, and listed off reasons why I should keep thinking of myself as a dynamic, physical being. I couldn't really hear him at the time, but he had planted a seed, for which I will always be grateful.

All I could think about was escaping from this medical prison and sleeping in my own bed.

It may surprise you to learn that the worst day of my life wasn't the day I fell and broke my back, or the day a doctor callously sneered as he told me I'd never walk again – it was the day I came home. This was a moment I had desperately looked forward to for every waking minute I spent wearing hospital pyjamas. But as soon as I was wheeled through our front door, I realised nothing would ever be the same again.

My wheelchair lowered my eyeline dramatically, and from where I sat it didn't even look or feel like my home any more. It all seemed odd, different somehow, like a movie set or a bad simulation. But I was the one who had changed. I wasn't the same woman who had lovingly made this house a home.

All the little things that were once part of everyday life – caring for my young children, taking pride in my home, sharing special moments with my husband – all of it was gone. I couldn't buy groceries; I couldn't even reach the floor, let alone pick up the boys' dirty clothes and beach towels. I couldn't taste anything, so how could I prepare a meal that anyone could stomach?

My disability dislocated me from my own family. I was a stranger in
my own home. For the first time in more than half a year, I was the only
wheelchair-bound person in the room and I felt like a freak show on
wheels. I never dreamed I'd miss the hideous spinal rehab unit, but I did.

When my seven-year-old was sick in bed, vomiting and crying, calling
out for his dad to help him and not for me, I felt I had failed as a mother
and I cried myself to sleep that night with tears of guilt and shame.

Our home still sat on a sunny green hill overlooking the sea, but inside
each room a dark fog of misery and gloom began to spread, and I was
the coal-black heart of it. For a time, I was so filled with irrational
anger that I hated the entire country of Thailand; it got so ridiculous
that I couldn't even think about ordering a takeaway dinner from
the local Thai restaurant without becoming upset.

I did my best to not gaze out any of the windows in our house that,
cruelly enough, directly overlook my favourite surf spot. Just seeing
a girl running down the road with a surfboard under her arm would
make me want to scream my lungs out.

I was losing my mind.

I hated waking up – and when I finally did open my eyes, I would ask to be taken to the bathroom where I would sit beneath a running shower for almost an hour, just so my family couldn't see my tears. I would close my eyes tight, and do my best to imagine I was surfing again, that the shower was the spray of a breaking wave washing over me … But this illusion never lasted long. Dragged screaming back into my living nightmare, I would punch the walls and the tears would begin again.

People who felt they knew more than I did kept telling me things would start to get easier, but it never did. Not having any abdominal muscle control, I couldn't transfer myself into or out of my wheelchair, use the bathroom, or even sit up without help. Cam had to turn me over at least three times during the night, every night, to prevent pressure injuries.

And if Cam had to go to work early, my youngest son, only a few years out of nappies himself, would help me pull up my underpants and jeans. I was completely dependent upon other people – I was a burden to those I loved most.

I was no longer my own person.

In addition to the dreadful limitations of my injuries, and the humiliation of my daily care, I was also in constant pain. Virtually every person I've spoken with since the accident confessed that they didn't know that most spinal cord injury survivors still felt pain in the affected parts of their body – I guess they imagine us sitting happily benumbed in our wheelchairs like dozy koalas wedged into a gumtree for twenty hours a day. Sadly, that is not the case at all.

Damaged nerves fired jarring sensations along the titanium rods screwed into my spine. Agonising bee-sting sensations erupted along the break-line around my chest. And the cruellest irony of all was the excruciating waves of burning phantom pains that overwhelmed my otherwise dead and useless torso, legs and feet.

This wasn't me. This wasn't my life. This could not possibly be my fate.

As an active, athletic, independent woman, I simply could not come to terms with what had befallen me.

I was in hell.

It was as if my soul was allergic to sunlight and affection. I hid from lifelong friends, and spurned the loving gestures of well-intentioned acquaintances and neighbours. And the more I rejected the world, the smaller my life became. At my lowest point, I distanced myself from my best friend, Bron, before cutting her off completely.

Bron is the most wonderful, loving person I know, and we had done everything together since we first met in the fifth grade. We had no secrets and a lifetime of shared history. We'd travelled the wilds, been each other's 'plus one' at a thousand parties, studied nursing together, surfed together and cared for each other's children.

As soon as she'd heard of my accident, Bron had instantly dropped everything to be at my bedside in Thailand, and she'd visited me faithfully in Royal North Shore Hospital as well. She was always there for me, and never said the wrong thing. She was my guardian angel. And I rejected her.

This will sound insane, because it is, but seeing Bron's beautiful face made me hate myself even more. I couldn't stand her looking at me, I couldn't bear her kindness. She was an ambassador of love from a time that was lost to me, a time I wanted to return to more than I had ever wanted anything in my entire life. In my fractured mind, my best friend was reduced to a living symbol of what my life could have been, and everything that it wasn't.

Pushing Bron away is one of my greatest regrets.

When I tell you that I frequently thought about suicide, I don't mean every other week, or even every other day. I mean almost every hour of every day. And were it not for my children, I would have almost certainly gone through with it.

I know Cam would have understood. He wouldn't want me to suffer, and he knows how important my freedom is to me. But my three little boys – I just couldn't inflict this additional horror upon them during this crucial formative stage of their lives, especially after all they'd already been put through because of me.

Re-reading my personal diary today, I'm shocked to see my careful planning process to determine exactly when I could take my own life with the least negative impact on those I loved most. My strategy was to identify the optimal suicide year that was far enough in the future that my sons would be emotionally mature enough to deal with this terrible loss, yet early enough so that my husband would still be sufficiently young and handsome to find love and start again.

That's not an easy sweet spot to find.

At this point, pain and despair had placed me beyond the reach of any human connection. There was no therapist, counsellor, fellow patient, well-meaning friend or family member who could get through to me, let alone help me.

The core of my being had collapsed, I had reached the final stages of depression, everything life offered me tasted like dust and I just wanted my misery to end.

I felt reduced to a wholly dependent lump of meat waiting for the life-support switch to be turned off.

In a way, I had already died.

But then a small bird brought me back to life.

My emotional breakthrough came when we rescued Penguin – an injured baby magpie that was blown out of her nest outside my mum's house.

How this tiny bundle of bone and feathers survived her twenty-metre fall from a towering Norfolk pine onto a bitumen car park, I do not know. But I'll never forget her wobbly head, the funny angle of her damaged wing, or feeling her tiny heart beating against the palm of my hand.

Here was a broken, fragile creature that needed help. And in that instant, I stopped thinking about myself, and my instincts as a mother and a nurse kicked back in. To this day, I remain astonished that two shiny eyes and a few grams of fluff could rescue me from bitter oblivion and help save my family, but that is exactly what happened.

Almost as soon as Penguin arrived in our home, the dark cloud started to lift. Shoving food into that greedy little beak without getting our fingers nipped united us with a common goal – the boys and I finally had something to talk about that made us happy.

Seeing that adorably ugly and often grubby little face also helped me remember how to smile for perhaps the first time since my accident. Instead of sobbing in the shower, there was laughter again.

It wasn't all smooth sailing. There were plenty of sleepless nights when Penguin was sick, and it was an enormous effort to make sure all her needs were met around the clock. But we loved this little bird and she loved us.

At no time was Penguin kept in a cage. She was always free to leave. But she chose to stay with us. We were more than free food and a warm bed to her. We were family. I thought of her as one of my own children and, at other times, as something like a sister.

Just as I worried about Penguin when her health or injuries seemed too great, Penguin somehow knew when I was hurting or feeling down, and would try her best to cheer me up. She would chat away and sing her heart out to me. Sometimes she'd just be a happy nuisance, which provided a welcome distraction, gently forcing me to acknowledge there was still plenty of happiness and beauty in my seemingly grey and gloomy world.

Penguin never blushed when I cursed and complained about my situation, making her the best sounding board ever. And of course, speaking aloud your fears reduces the potency of their venom. What a funny pair we must have seemed, talking, swearing and singing to each other for hours on end. And then sometimes, when it was all too much to bear, we would lie down outside together and just stare up at the sky, hoping and wishing for better days ahead.

Look, I'm not saying Penguin was an angel – she pooed on the dining table and our white sofa cushions far too often for that – but whenever she appeared, my mood lifted and she always made me smile. I know her damaged wing caused her great pain, but she never gave up trying to fly. I can't recall how many times I caught my breath as she launched herself awkwardly into the air off the furniture and flap-slammed into the nearest wall like a drunk feather duster.

And when she finally overcame all her injuries and flew for the very first time, my heart soared. Her maiden voyage took place in our living room, to the delight of our whole family. Shortly after that, she flew outside and took to the wild skies as if she was born for this – which, of course, she was. It was the happiest I'd felt in forever.

Penguin was living proof that – with enough love, support and hard work – hope can become reality. And by caring for Penguin, by giving her all the love and dedication I could, I was suddenly able to understand what my family and closest friends had been telling me all along – I was not useless, I could make a difference, and therefore my life still had meaning and purpose.

Watching Penguin fly each day motivated me to invest more energy in my own physical recovery on a daily basis. I started looking for ways to get stronger, fitter and more flexible. Likewise, Penguin's squawks and melodies encouraged me to be more vocal about what I needed and wanted, and showed me the value in sharing positive thoughts and feelings with others. I determined I would complain only as much as Penguin did, which was never.

Penguin stayed by my side almost constantly, keeping watch over me and my precious family. When strangers knocked at the door, or well-meaning but thoughtless and irksome do-gooders intruded on my personal space, she would make it clear they were not wanted. On one occasion, she chased a disrespectful nurse out the door during a house call.

Penguin was my champion; she always wanted what was best for me, which is why she wouldn't allow me to wallow in self-pity. She constantly provoked me to be active and shamed me by her own tireless example. As she grew stronger, so did I. We shared each other's victories, large and small.

The same little magpie that was barely clinging to life when we found her had become our fierce and loving protector, and my true inspiration. With her glossy feathers and bright beak, I would be tempted to call her a sky goddess were it not for the unholy mess she made around the house, and the countless times she pecked and scratched her big brothers or snatched the teabag right out of my cup.

Penguin's complete transformation became a daily reminder that we are not our past, no matter how traumatic or life-changing it might have been. While it was probably obvious to everyone else, I didn't initially realise that by helping Penguin heal, I was helping myself to heal. I thought I was saving her life, but she was saving mine.

Caring for that silly little bird gave me purpose and made me happy, and this allowed me to tackle more difficult tasks with a positive mindset. Unlike most people, I don't wake up wondering whether my day is going to be good or bad. It is always going to be bad unless I actively do something to make it good. And nothing feels as good as helping others.

Penguin did something no doctor could: she got me off my paralysed bum (figuratively speaking).

She also taught me how to be a better person.

Scrambling after Penguin gave me back some of my velocity and, in time, I also became a little more confident in social settings. I began listening to Cam's constant encouragement and agreed to try new things. Sometimes it worked out, and sometimes it didn't, but at least it got me out of the house.

I continued to avoid my old friends; I simply felt more comfortable in the company of people who never knew me before I was paralysed. As far as they were concerned, I was born in a wheelchair, and that suited me fine. I hated people reminding me of who I used to be, and I was still too fragile to deal with insensitive questions or unfiltered pity.

People are strange – so often we forget the impact of our words, especially when our curiosity exceeds our compassion. I learned the hard way that even the nicest person can be oblivious to the suffering of others and unintentionally hurtful. Most often, people ignore you rather than risk a difficult encounter, but sometimes they choose only to see a 'cripple in a wheelchair', not an individual struggling to do the best they can in a terrible situation. For some folk, a wheelchair awakens a gleeful inquisitiveness born of dread, and seems to invite the most tone-deaf and offensively probing and personal questions that no one would otherwise dream of asking. For example:

Question: How do you go to the toilet?
Answer: In pretty much the same way as a patient on a hospital ward or in a nursing home, but how is this private matter any of your business?

Question: What are you hoping for in terms of your recovery?
Answer: I'm hoping the ghost of David Bowie will appear by my bedside and touch my severed spinal cord and make me whole again.

Question: What do you miss the most?
Answer: Walking, bladder control and orgasms … not always in that order.

Question: Would you like me and my family to pray for you?
Answer: That would be really nice, thank you, but I'd be very grateful if your family would also consider making a donation to SpinalCure Australia. The fact is that spinal cord injury will be cured one day, and that day is getting closer and closer. Already great progress is being made with the repair of other complex nerve injuries. Before the discovery of penicillin, people used to have limbs amputated and even die from tiny splinters. One day, the treatment of nerve repair may be almost as simple as prescribing a course of antibiotics. I know that the medical scientists who are actively searching for a cure for spinal cord injury at SpinalCure Australia genuinely appreciate your prayers, but your donation will keep the lights on while they work.

Question: Do you sometimes feel it might have been better if you'd died?
Answer: I certainly wish one of us was dead.

Question: Looking back, what positives have come from being paralysed?
Answer: Nothing. Zero. Not a biscuit.

Okay, I never really said any of those replies at the time, but I kind of wish I had, instead of shrivelling up in mortified silence. Also, my last imaginary answer is only half-true. I wouldn't wish my disability on anyone for even a single minute; constant suffering has not made me a better person. However, it has given me a new perspective on humanity, and here's what I see:

There are a great many thoughtless people on the planet. People who seem decent on the surface, but are so caught up in their own lives that they can't see how others are broken and hurting, and who aren't prepared to make any meaningful effort to change their words or actions to benefit anyone but themselves. Catholics would call this a 'sin of omission', but I'm not a Catholic, so I just say that they have their heads up their own arses and this makes them unspeakably cruel.

This was me at my lowest point, when both my body and spirit were broken.

Likewise, there are gloomy jerks aplenty who refuse to accept even the smallest amount of the endless love and beauty that this world has to offer. Such wilful self-sabotage makes them their own worst enemies and a burden to others.

Yep, definitely me.

But there are also others, so many others, who are so incredibly kind and giving that they restore your faith in humanity and in all living things. Before my accident, I was a true optimist. I already knew there were lots of good people in the world, but even I had no idea that so many truly good people existed. People who look past their own problems to help others even less fortunate. Ordinary men and women who commit acts of extraordinary selflessness every single day and seek nothing in return. Those who take the best of themselves and share this with as many people as they can.

That's who I am trying to be.

Penguin opened my eyes and my heart. She helped me to be my best self, or at least my worst self far less often.

I didn't have Penguin's energy, but I did whatever I could to be physically and mentally active and it made me feel better about almost everything. I was better able to face the setbacks and challenges that used to overwhelm me with pain, anger and despair. The idea of fresh air plus physical and mental exercise being good for your wellbeing is not remotely original, I know, but it made a huge difference to me.

With consistent effort, I slowly, and I do mean slowly, became stronger in both mind and body. In time, I was open to new challenges, which led to newfound happiness, even though not all of them proved successful initially.

For example, I was dying to get back into the ocean, to return to my happy place, but sadly it didn't go well the first time. I felt distressed in the water almost immediately. Without the use of my legs, I found it hard to stay upright – even the smallest swell tossed me around. I couldn't dive under waves, push through whitewash or fight the current, and my confidence sunk like a stone.

Without control over my chest muscles, I couldn't tolerate the weight of the sea on my lungs, and breathing was extremely difficult. The muscles in my torso spasmed, painful involuntary contractions that caught me unawares. I could almost feel those spinal board straps tightening around my ribs again, and the horrible sensation frightened and upset me. I pleaded with Cam to take me straight home.

It's a tough moment when you realise your sanctuary has turned against you.

If getting into the water was too much for me, I thought maybe I could still have fun on top of it, so I tried kayaking – a suggestion first made to me back in spinal rehab, and championed by my wonderful husband who refused to give up on me.

At first, it was very unnerving, I'm not going to lie. I had visions of myself drowning while strapped in to an upside-down kayak. But as I got the hang of it, and began to glide across Narrabeen Lakes with comparative ease, I realised I'd found something that truly made me feel alive again.

Kayaking really worked for me on a physical level, even though I could only paddle with my arms and shoulders; my strength, endurance, flexibility and balance improved dramatically. But more than that, the exertion helped me sweat out a few demons and the stunning views themselves were the best therapy I've ever had, and gifted me true peace of mind. Being out on the water freed me from my personal prison on wheels – I was back in nature again and under my own power.

I was my own person again.

My dad's belief that the greatest reward for hard work is getting to enjoy the sunshine was proven true – and after winning two state titles and two national titles, I was selected for the Australian Paracanoe Team and travelled to Italy for the World Championships. This was a wonderful experience, not just because it was my first international trip since Thailand, but because Cam brought our boys to join me for a post-competition holiday in Rome – the same place where our romantic globetrotting adventures first began some twenty years earlier.

By the time we got home from Italy, Penguin had moved on. She had matured and it was time for her to establish her own nest and territory elsewhere. We missed her terribly, and still do, but I am so happy she has finally found her place in the world, and so grateful to her for helping me find mine.

We have rescued and rehabilitated many injured and orphaned birds since we took Penguin in, but there will never be another like her. Penguin entered and exited our lives at precisely the right time. I'm not always the most spiritual person, but if you told me Penguin was an angel in disguise, I'd probably believe you. But then again, I'd also want to know why an angel kept pooing on my white sofa cushions!

While I loved the excitement of elite kayak competitions, the truth is that I just wanted to get back in the water; I wanted to feel like my old self again. To me, the biggest win from kayaking was not any particular race victory, it was becoming strong enough and brave enough to get back into the ocean, which I finally did. And now, after years of believing I'd never surf again, I'm finally back on a surfboard, where I belong.

It's not perfect, not by a long way – I'm now lying down instead of standing up, my turning is limited and I need to be pushed onto a wave by someone else – but surfing in any fashion with my husband and our children fills me with joy and it's brought our family even closer, so I'm not complaining.

Thanks to Penguin, I stopped looking inward, reliving my fears, mistakes and regrets, and instead tried to turn my gaze to the world around me, appreciating everyday beauty and wonder, as well as acknowledging the hardships other people face. Just because someone is not stuck in a wheelchair doesn't mean they are guaranteed an easy or happy life.

Thanks to Penguin, I don't dwell so much on what I can't do; instead, I look for things I can do. And I also look for things I can do for others. Most importantly, Penguin taught me that just because something looks hopeless, it doesn't mean that it is.

The full story of Penguin was too special to keep to ourselves, which is why we shared it in the book *Penguin Bloom*; perhaps you've already read it. I assume a great many people must have because I receive lovely emails from readers all around the world on a daily basis.

Truth be told, I was a little reluctant to join in the creative process at first – I wasn't quite ready to open up, to revisit all the horrible moments I wanted to forget. It wasn't until a month or so after Cam and the writer, our dear friend Bradley Trevor Greive, had started working on the book that I finally spoke to BTG at length about what I'd been through. But once I started, it got easier. I could feel my weighty emotional armour falling away and I didn't want to stop – I shared my private diary and revealed hopes and fears that had only ever been spoken aloud in front of Penguin. I would Skype with BTG for hours each day, almost two thousand hours that first year, as he tried his best to get inside my cracked head to understand as much as he could about what it meant to be me, and I did my best to describe the indescribable about being paralysed.

Having endured twenty surgeries of his own, BTG had great empathy for my condition, but we soon delved into territory that is wholly unknown to anyone who has not suffered a spinal cord injury, and so many of our conversations were very difficult for both of us. Talking about the hardship I had faced, and was still facing, made my paralysis and phantom pains feel unbearably fresh. It was tough to pick myself back up after discussing certain topics, and sometimes I couldn't sleep afterward – hideous nightmares returned as I wrenched open old wounds. Some days, exhausted by an in-depth conversation about my disabilities, I would ask Cam to help me up onto the trampoline in the front yard, where I would lie down for the rest of the afternoon. Penguin would often sit by my side or perch protectively on top of my aching head, like a soothing heat-pack.

But there was an upside as well. I started recalling all the happy memories before and after my accident. I began to acknowledge and better appreciate the roles played by Penguin and my family and so many friends and strangers who had helped me move forward with my life. I also saw clearly, for perhaps the first time, how far I'd come since my accident in Thailand. I am not suggesting that collaborating on a book is a clinically proven form of trauma therapy, but it did help me unravel an ugly knot of memories and emotions, as well as remind me that I am still in control of my own life narrative.

The finished book was a thing of beauty. Honest, raw and heartfelt – a visual love-letter from my husband, and so much more. I felt deeply moved when I first read it, and I still do. But as wonderful as our book was, and is, nothing prepared me for the reception it received when it was published, partly because it still felt like a very personal project far more than any kind of public statement. Whenever I'd thought of people reading it, I felt conflicted; I was genuinely proud of what we had created, but it was still a little unnerving to imagine people reading such intimate details. It was as if guests had arrived at my home while all my underwear was hanging on the clothesline.

The attention we received was overwhelming, but in a really unexpected way. As a shy person I prefer being invisible in public, even more so since my accident, and it was hard to adjust to people recognising me, let alone seeking me out. But I started noticing a lovely shift in the way strangers addressed me – instead of sympathy, I received gratitude. Instead of tiptoeing around my situation, or burying me in saccharine platitudes and pity, people started to thank me for sharing my story. They would tell me how reading about our experiences had helped them, or someone they loved. This response was everything we'd hoped for.

And then it all went a bit mad.

Photographers, filmmakers and journalists from all around the world arrived on our doorstep, hoping to talk to us and meet Penguin. Spinal cord injury charities that we supported asked us to be even more involved. Fellow survivors reached out for advice or wanted me to teach them how to kayak, long-lost friends wanted to reconnect, and there was an endless parade of well-wishers. Bizarrely, all of this was absolutely fine with me. I found some media interviews a little stressful, as I hate being in the spotlight, but so long as their attention focused on the book, on Penguin, and on raising awareness and money for charity, I was better than all right. The one and only request that nearly undid me was being asked to speak in public.

At first, I did basic question-and-answer sessions with fellow survivors and medical staff at hospitals and spinal rehab units, then with small groups at bookstores, and finally with larger audiences at literary festivals. Cam was with me on every occasion and he helped me get through each event without panicking.

But when it came time for my first solo presentation, a one-hour speech to a large crowd, it was a very different thing altogether. No matter how frequently I rehearsed my presentation, I couldn't calm my nerves. On the morning of my talk I felt physically ill, and in the minutes before going on stage my hands were shaking and I wanted to vomit. Despite weeks of preparation, I broke down at the end of my speech, choking on the words, my eyes filling with tears. I was embarrassed, but when the houselights came up, I saw that the audience was weeping with me.

I would never have dreamed of attempting public speaking before my accident, before Penguin. Talking to just one person at a time was always difficult for me, and two people at once made me a nervous wreck. But while facing a crowded room terrified me, I immediately realised it was a powerful way to share what I had learned, and I was determined to get better at it. But I also knew I had a long way to go.

This brings me to the moment when I decided I would tell my story in this book. Well, it was actually the combination of two moments, just over two years apart.

The first took place in winter, a year after Penguin's departure, during a welcome family escape to a friend's cottage just beyond the Blue Mountains. As soon as we arrived, we unpacked and then started exploring the nearby farms. I was also taken for my very first ride on a quadbike, which was great fun. By the time we got back, it was almost dark. The weather forecast said it might snow and I was chilled to my bones. Fortunately, our little home-away-from-home had a cute combustion stove fireplace, and the boys quickly loaded it with kindling and had it burning brightly. Soon I was sitting by the fire, sipping a cup of hot tea, feeling incredibly cosy and grateful. It was just what I needed.

Later that evening, when it was time for bed, Cam was helping me undress for my shower when suddenly he stopped taking off my mud-spattered jeans, his eyes grew wide and he muttered a grim 'oh no'. My left leg was crimson and swollen, as if badly sunburned, and immediately we both knew I'd been sitting too close to the fireplace. The instant and deeply unpleasant realisation we shared was that this was not even the leg closest to the flames, so we prepared ourselves for the worst, which was just as well.

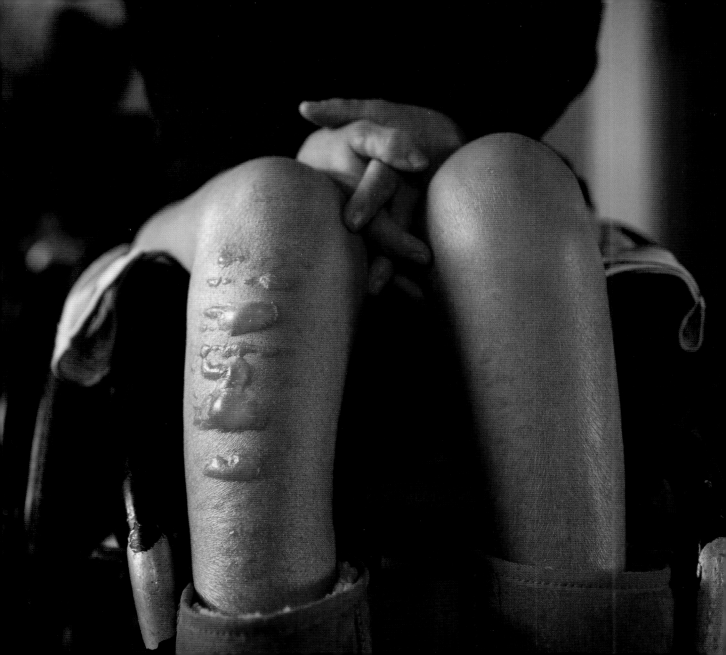

As Cam carefully and slowly pulled down the denim on my right leg, it looked very ugly. The heat from the fire had brutally scorched my flesh, inflicting third-degree burns to my lower leg. Once again, I was driven to hospital on the first day of our family holiday, this time to receive a second skin graft.

I felt so stupid and helpless, a pitiful burden on my family and a dangerous menace to myself. When the hospital sent me home, I was forbidden from doing any exercise or getting wet – I was a miserable shut-in once again, and I had a gift for making everyone else miserable as well. Was this all I had to look forward to – endless injuries and health problems? I could easily imagine how gutted I would feel if one day neurosurgeons were able to repair my spinal cord so that I could walk again, but my legs were already amputated due to complications with disfiguring wounds like these. Right on cue, suicidal thoughts flooded my mind.

Eighteen months later, in summer, I was on the beach, being helped onto a small wave by one of our neighbours, former two-time surfing world champion Tom Carroll. Nola Wilson, the mother of pro-surfer Julian Wilson, had written me a heartfelt letter to try to convince me to get back into the surf, and I found her words so compelling I'd agreed to give it another go. Cam had seized the initiative and organised a modified surfboard, Tom volunteered to help get me going, and we all held our collective breath as the wave pitched me forward and off I went.

To my surprise, I loved it – my mind still knew how to read the waves, even if my body didn't. Not long after that, I entered my first surfing contest, just for fun. I was a little frightened and I didn't win, but I came close, I had a great time and I met some wonderful people who have since become my friends.

Two months later, I received a surprise email from Surfing Australia, letting me know I'd been selected as a member of the Australian Adaptive Surfing Team and that I was invited to compete at the World Championships held in San Diego, USA.

I was over the moon and so was my family – the boys and I had never been to America before. I trained every day, in the surf and in the gym. Cam and I were worried we couldn't afford the trip, but several generous Australian companies pitched in to make sure I had absolutely everything I needed to compete at the highest level. This was really happening. I was pumped.

The sun was shining when we touched down in San Diego, and it just got better from there. The local event organisers were amazing hosts, my Aussie team members were super fun and highly motivated and, except for a few choppy afternoons, the surfing conditions suited me perfectly all week. On the final day of the contest, I was crowned world champion.

As I rode my final wave in to shore, everyone on the beach was cheering. My team carried me out of the water on my board and held me aloft like an emperor – or a half-drowned human sacrifice, take your pick. When I spotted my three boys, they were all smiling from ear to ear. The look of joy and pride on their faces is an image I will cherish forever.

Becoming world champion was amazing, but still being able to do something that makes my children proud of me was the most incredible feeling in the world. If you'd told me that this is where I'd be two years earlier, when the doctors were peeling skin off my thigh to giftwrap my roasted shin, I'd never have believed you.

Frequent lows and rare highs – gravel and diamonds – that's what almost everyone's life journey looks like, and mine is no exception. Perhaps my lows are a little lower than most, but maybe some of my highs are a little higher as well, who's to say? When I look back at my path from despair to delight, I'm shocked that so much can change for the better in such a relatively short time.

And this realisation is what inspired me to share my story with you in this book. You see, when I broke my back there were two things I desperately wanted to believe, needed to believe in fact, in order to keep going. The first was that medical scientists were fully committed to finding a way to repair my spinal cord so that one day I'll be able to stand on my own two feet again. The second was that my awful new life could somehow get better than it was, not just be tolerable, but reach a point where I could find genuine purpose and enjoyment and once again be proud of who I am.

Well, here's what I know to be true.

No matter how low you are feeling right now, for whatever reason, I promise you that your life will get better. It will take time and effort and self-belief, but it will get better. There will be days when your soul is spent and all seems lost, but it will get better. There may never be a time when you are free from pain, but it will get better.

Don't get me wrong, I am still not at peace with my disability. And I don't think I ever will be.

I am definitely not a better person because of my accident. I haven't attained a higher intellectual or spiritual plane, I am not one with the universe and I am not one with my wheelchair. When I hear someone chirping about living without any regrets, I roll my eyes and whisper 'bullshit' under my breath.

Life is many things all at once, and some of those things suck. Plain and simple. The remedy, to the degree that any exists, is to not let the misery of the bad prevent you from enjoying the good. And while that is far easier said than done, this is exactly how I can hate being paralysed and still be grateful to be alive. I can be deeply unhappy about my pain and disability and still be capable of great happiness. I can feel ashamed of myself for pushing my best friend away when I was depressed and I can enjoy rebuilding that friendship. I can regret the tragedy that befell my family in Thailand seven years ago and still look forward to what life has to offer. I don't know that 'balance' is the right word, but it's not all or nothing. Life is always a blend of good and bad, and while I don't pretend I'm not hurting, I can still find joy and meaning in my life.

And it's working. I'm happier today than I have been in many years. I'm the best me I've been in a long time. But even on my best days, there are moments of sadness. There are very few mornings when I wake up feeling amazing – almost none, in fact. This is largely because I'm in constant pain, and because no one likes looking at twisted lifeless limbs before breakfast. And also because there are nights when I even dream about being stuck in a wheelchair, which always brings me down.

And then there are the nights where I dream about being the woman I used to be, about what she would be doing now if she was here instead of me. It's so beautiful and exciting … and then when I open my eyes and look in the mirror and see that I'm not her – it's hard. It's very hard. Because while I may not look like the strong, confident young woman who once trekked through the Simien Mountains in Ethiopia, in my heart I am still her. I still want everything she wants. Far more than she does.

But while I don't always see my true self in the mirror, I see it in the eyes of my husband and our boys, who are all strong, loving, brave, compassionate, creative souls, who actively try to change the world for the better.

And if I falter, and I start to slip backward, which happens often, I ask for help. I would be dead if people hadn't helped me.

And so now I also want to be able to help others.

I have three boys who need me and I am not about to quit on them. I have a husband who loves me, and I want to be there for him in any way I can. I am very grateful to the medical staff who saved my life, and I owe a massive debt to my family and friends whose love, patience and encouragement helped me move forward when I felt I couldn't go on, and I want to express my eternal gratitude in a meaningful way.

And, thanks to the success of *Penguin Bloom*, I've been contacted by people all over the world who have also suffered a spinal cord injury, or perhaps some other terrible tragedy, who are looking for help to navigate through their worst nightmare, and I want to do my best for them as well.

There's no magic trick, no short cut, no secret recipe. I just do what I can to pick myself up and try to make it work. It's not always pretty, but it's got me this far and I'm not stopping now.

And when I hit rock bottom and start to feel sorry for myself, as I often do, I think back to my first journey across Africa …

As I mentioned near the beginning of my story, I took my very first trip to West Africa on my own. I left my job as Lord Denning's private nurse and flew from London, England, to Dakar, Senegal, where I joined an overland expedition that was travelling across the continent by truck.

It doesn't matter whether you go to the edge of the world or even beyond, you'll always find a few fun-loving Aussies waiting for you, and Dakar was no different. There were a number of young Australian travellers already signed on, and I quickly bonded with all of them, including a sweet and funny twenty-six-year-old from rural New South Wales named Antony who, like me, had recently found work in London. Ant's lifelong dream was to see Uganda's famous mountain gorillas. He was so excited knowing that in just a few weeks or so, he was finally going to make this a reality.

It wasn't the most comfortable journey, bouncing endlessly along bumpy unsealed roads and narrow potholed highways, but thankfully my bottom was plumped up from English cooking and up for the adventure. I loved exploring the cities and villages, soaking in everything that was new to me. I loved speaking with local people, using the clumsy schoolgirl French that I'd learned just for this journey. I loved sitting on the long bench-seats running along the sides of the truck as we roared through the countryside, waving to everyone like happy idiots. I felt like I was driving through the pages of *National Geographic* magazine. Bob Marley always seemed to be playing on the radio. I loved everything.

After leaving Senegal, we enjoyed a brief excursion to Mauritania and then travelled to Mali, which remains a favourite of mine. In the historic city of Djenné, we were welcomed by local Fulani women, who were gorgeous and full of laughter. Their children thought a tiny Australian girl was the perfect playmate, and I did my best to prove them right. Our route eastward took us toward the northernmost bend of the Niger River, and the southernmost fringe of the Sahara Desert. Two Tuareg men wearing traditional blue robes, their heads and faces covered by indigo tagelmusts, suddenly appeared out of the dunes astride golden camels, stared right through us, and vanished just as quickly. Then we got blasted from every direction by a massive sandstorm. I was in heaven.

Our next destination was Burkina Faso, a West African country whose name literally translates to 'the land of incorruptible men', which makes it hilariously ironic that this is where my daypack, containing my camera, wallet and traveller's cheques, was stolen. All the money I had earned in England was gone.

I was feeling down and out in the middle of nowhere, as there was no way I could complete my trans-African road trip. Thankfully, I was able to continue on with the group through the Ivory Coast and Ghana, as I had prepaid for those legs, but when we reached Togo it was the end of the line for me. I had no choice but to fly back to London from Lomé–Tokoin International Airport.

As I said goodbye to Antony and my other travelling companions, who had all become close friends, I promised them I'd get another job and save up as quickly as I could and try my best to meet up with them somewhere in East Africa in a month or two. It broke my heart to watch that old truck rumble away into the distance without me.

While I returned to private nursing in England, Ant and our intrepid friends travelled on to Benin, Nigeria, Cameroon, Central African Republic, Congo and then, at long last, Uganda.

When the truck crossed the Congolese border and arrived in Arua, Uganda, I'm told Ant could hardly contain himself, knowing that very soon he would finally see his beloved mountain gorillas in the wild. Apparently, it was all he could talk about over dinner that evening and even afterward, while washing dishes in huge, colourful plastic tubs set up on the wooden folding tables beside the truck.

Ant had such a good heart and a truly wonderful sense of humour – in my mind I can clearly see him laughing, his eyes shining as he scrubbed pots and dried plates with his fellow adventurers. But at that moment, violent terrorists – local rebels or possibly a paramilitary unit from neighbouring Rwanda – threw a hand grenade at my friends and it exploded right where Antony stood.

Ant bled to death on the way to hospital that night.

He never saw a mountain gorilla.

He never turned twenty-seven.

His killers were never identified or brought to justice.

I think about Ant whenever I feel like surrendering to self-pity. I still cry every time. Tears of loss and gratitude.

It's not just because I would also have likely been badly injured or killed in that same murderous blast had I still been on the expedition with my friends, though I certainly appreciate that fact.

It's that I am staggered with grief for Ant, and for all the young men and women and children who lose their lives every day, before they've had a chance to attempt anything they dreamed of doing in this life, to realise their potential, to find their passion, to experience a fraction of the things that I have seen and done.

I know what true suffering feels like, but who am I to complain about how I am forced to live, when Antony, his family, his girlfriend, and all those who knew and loved him would give all they have for him to still be alive, or even to have lived just one more year, one more month, one more week, one more day?

Falling off a balcony doesn't give me the right to give you advice on anything beyond the importance of not leaning against safety barriers, and I don't pretend otherwise.

Nor can I teach you how to overcome pain and depression, because I'm still in pain and I continue to have my share of dark days. But if you'll indulge me, I'd like to remind you of something you've always known to be true.

Life is a fragile and precious thing.

Anything and everything can be taken away from you when you least expect it, through no fault of your own.

And you don't have to suffer a terrible accident like I did to feel lost, invisible, unlovable or broken. We all face different challenges every day, and life can be hard and painful for anyone.

Regardless of what happened to you and how much of your life you feel is missing, fight for whatever is left.

Go where your heart calls you. Tell people that you love them.

And when life seems unbearable, do your best to remain open to love, even if it's from a scruffy little magpie.

It's not easy, but it makes all the difference.

Trust me, I know.

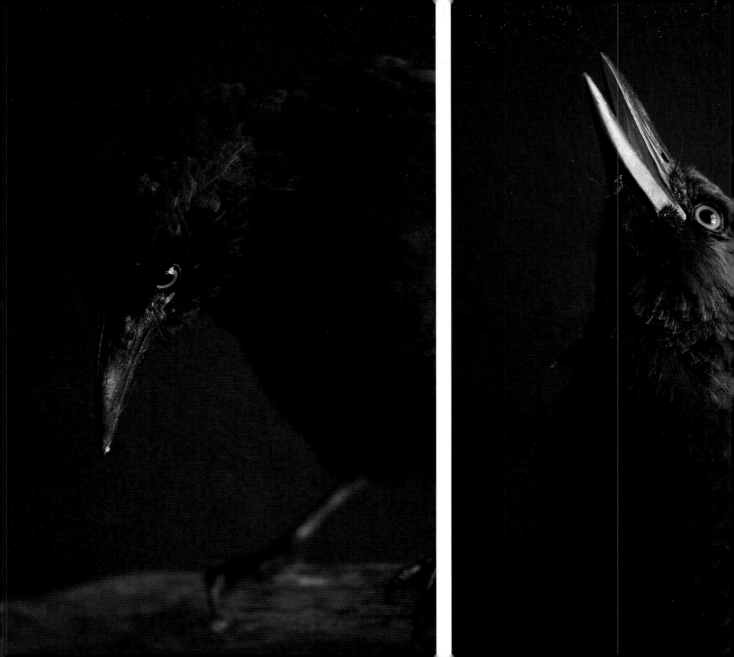

When I wake up each morning, I die a little bit.

No matter how hard I try not to, I always think about before.
When I was me.

I mourn the life that was taken from me, stolen from my family.
It still seems impossible that it all came to this.

… But then I think about Lord Denning grieving for his wife and
siblings, I think about all the young girls in Ethiopia desperate
for Dr Catherine Hamlin's help, I think about the broken young
men I met during spinal rehab, and I think about Antony's
unfulfilled dreams.

And then I start living.

For them.

For my family and friends.

For everyone I've ever met or might one day meet.

For myself.

Because you're never too old, or too damaged, or too lost to experience the joy and wonder of this world, and to do and say the things that matter most.

As long as you are alive, your dreams are alive.

That's enough for me.

Sam Bloom

Epilogue

A letter to my three beautiful boys

Dearest Rueben, Noah and Oli,

I'm so sorry. It wasn't supposed to be like this.

'Hate' is such an ugly word, but nothing else seems to describe how I feel about being paralysed. I truly hate not being able to stand, or to walk, or to run down to the beach and surf together like we used to. I hate feeling that two-thirds of my body has completely switched off for good. But what I hate most of all is I'm not the mother I once was, I'm not the mother I want to be, and I'm definitely not the mother you deserve.

We were all so happy before – I never imagined that life could be so perfect. And if I ever took it for granted then, well, I certainly know better now. Each of you was so special and unique and utterly wonderful from the moment you were born. Rueben, you were adorably chatty and outgoing, all creativity and mischief, and a natural comedian. Always thinking, always moving, it was almost impossible to keep up with you. Noah, you were a quiet, thoughtful baby, but only until Aretha Franklin came on, and then your little head would start bobbing and you'd start dancing, even when you were strapped into your car seat. And Oli, you were supremely easygoing and tough as teak, you never cried. You were a born explorer, boldly crawling and climbing where no one had crawled or climbed before. Your dad and I pulled you out of so many trees I thought we might be raising a hyperactive baby koala by mistake.

Every minute together was pure joy; I loved watching you open your eyes, staring all around, looking so adorably astonished as you made a thousand tiny discoveries before breakfast. I don't think anything sounds as lovely as hearing your children's laughter, or their first almost-words. Now that you're all grown up, so big and strong and wise to the world around you, it's hard to imagine you being so tiny and soft and new, but you were. And nothing ever felt better than holding you in my arms.

I honestly thought I knew what true happiness was before I became a mother, but I was so embarrassingly wrong. Your father and I travelled the world together when we were young, free and fearless, and head over heels in love – every day was an adventure that I never wanted to end. But through your eyes, I saw a different world altogether, a place more beautiful and precious than anything I can describe, and I found a whole other person within myself. The love and passion and strength you summoned from me felt like an enormous star growing inside my heart.

Even after an exhausting day of pooey nappies, teething tantrums, kitchen chaos and playtime mess, I never wanted to go to sleep in case I would miss you doing something for the first time. Every morning when I picked you up from your cots, I would notice small exquisite changes as your features become more distinctly your own and your little pink fingers grew stronger. You seemed to be growing by the minute and every breath and blink seemed somehow miraculous.

As each birthday came around, you did more and more to amaze me and make me proud. You drove me a little crazy as well, that's hardly a secret, but you also made all my motherhood dreams come true. And all I wanted, and still want, is for your childhood dreams to come true as well.

But then I fell, and I couldn't get up. I still can't. And because of my accident, instead of being a bright guiding light in your lives, I have cast a dark cloud over all of us for so many years. I feel terribly guilty that I have ruined your childhood.

My instinct as your mother is to care for you, no matter what, and it breaks my heart that instead you are forced to care for me. Don't get me wrong, I am so grateful for the love and compassion you give me each day, but I still weep with frustration that our natural roles of parent and child have been so cruelly reversed.

I am so desperately sorry for the sadness that I brought home from hospital with me. I try to shed the feelings of bitterness and dread, I try to be positive, I try to stay strong and put on a brave face, God knows I do … but you boys see through me every time and I know it hurts you deeply to see me suffering. I know my tears make you feel just as sad and helpless as I do, and that is the very opposite of what I want.

My love for you and my hopes for your future transcend any personal battle that I am facing. I want you to grow into brave, capable, loving young men – I want you to be happy and fearless, and always be true to who you are. You have made so many sacrifices for me, but now I want you to live boldly for me; I never want my wheelchair to be an anchor that holds you back from your best life.

As your mother, I want nothing so much as to cheer you on as you pursue your passions. Never give up on your dreams, promise me that you never will, and I promise you that I will never give up trying to walk again.

Your love has sustained me through the worst moments of my life – you have literally kept me alive. There were many times when I felt myself falling into the darkness and I wanted the pain to stop so badly that I didn't want to wake up ever again. But just when I was losing my grip on life, your perfect faces called me back to this world. My love for you sustained me when nothing else could reach me. I love you far too much to ever leave you behind.

I want you to know how proud I am of each of you and your special gifts – Rueben, with your woodwork, Noah, with your music, and Oli, with your freestyle scootering. I am so excited to imagine what your talents will accomplish, who you will love, and where your dreams will take you. I have seen a great deal of this amazing world, and I want you to see even more.

Life is not always fair, but it is still beautiful if you will just lift up your head and open your eyes. Life is not always easy, but it is always bearable, even when it seems like it isn't. And if you keep trying your best, you will eventually find yourself where you always wanted to be, doing what you always wanted to do, no matter what obstacles are in your way.

When I first came home from hospital, I couldn't bear to look at the sea, believing I would never surf again. But today we are surfing together; it's not quite how it once was, but it still feels wonderful to ride the waves with you again.

After flying home from Thailand for additional surgery, I never ever wanted to board another airplane; the memories of how my horrific accident ruined our first family holiday were utterly devastating. But a few years later, after countless hours of hard work in the gym and out on the water, I was on my way to Italy to compete in the Paracanoe World Championships and then enjoy a wonderful family holiday with you in Rome. Then we were in California, for the Adaptive Surfing World Championships, and to explore majestic Yosemite. Today, we travel all the time, wherever we want. I may not be living as I would like, but every year is a little better than the last, and therefore I'm able to look forward to even better days ahead with confidence.

I hate what has happened to me, I really do, I'm not going to pretend otherwise, but there is so much I love about my life, and I'm not giving up. My story isn't over yet. And your stories are just beginning.

Nothing matters more to me than for you to know that I love you dearly, and I always will. Please don't put your lives on hold for me, and do what makes you happy today, not tomorrow, as you never know what life has in store for you.

If something is important to you, don't let the naysayers get you down or break your spirit. Don't ever take 'no' or 'never' for an answer – in fact, put a big question mark on the end of every reason and excuse people use to tell you why you can't do something. Then commit yourself to working out exactly how you are going to accomplish the thing they said could never be achieved.

When a doctor told me I'd never walk again, I chose instead to focus on how I would walk again, how I can rebuild my body and improve my damaged nervous system, and how I can help find a cure for myself and others. And while on some days, my worst days, this seems impossible to me, I know that so many things in life seem impossible until someone asks how it can be done.

The 'how' is everything. Even though I'm not yet back on my feet, I'm determined to walk again, and working toward that seemingly impossible goal is why I'm so much stronger and happier than I was, and also why our life as a family has improved dramatically – and we're only just getting started. Being part of the 'how' is the key to being your best self, to making the world a little bit better and, just sometimes, to making the impossible possible.

And you don't have to do any of this alone. Your mum and dad will always be in your corner, and so will your brothers. Never forget that the world is full of smart, loving, wonderful people who are willing to help you. Accept their help and give back even more in return.

I can only imagine how frightening and upsetting it was for you to watch your mum get so badly injured. But don't let a freak accident taint your perception of what life has to offer. Instead, focus on the medical miracle that kept me alive, and the incredible love and support that we received when we really needed it.

Life can be hard, even awful at times, but the world is still filled with beauty and wonder. I know that's easy for me to say, living in Sydney's Northern Beaches, overlooking the Tasman Sea. Pretty much the worst thing that ever happened to our community was the time rough seas washed a dead whale into the ocean pool by the beach. But I've seen beauty and wonder elsewhere in abundance, and so have you. I have found kindness everywhere, and so have you. Yes, this world can break your heart, but it can also make it whole again.

Please don't take anything for granted; be attentive to the special details and do your best to appreciate the smallest pleasures and surprises in life, for they are the things you will miss most if you ever lose them. Trust me on that.

Be kind to everyone you meet, especially those who seem overwhelmed with anger, frustration or grief, because you cannot know what terrible burden they are struggling with. Your words and actions can make all the difference in the world to them. A single compassionate moment of your time could save a life.

Please love and support each other, as you always have, for while you are amazing individuals, you are so much stronger together. I don't doubt that the three of you could do absolutely anything you put your minds to.

And whenever you see me, or think of me, please remember me as I was before the accident, because that is how I want to feel, and one day that is how I want to be again. Know that I am trying my best to be the mother you deserve, I am fighting a daily battle with every ounce of strength and energy I have, and when, on my bad days, you see me struggling, the anguish on my face is because I am determined to make progress, and not because I am giving up. I will never give up on you, our family, or myself.

I miss Penguin dearly and I think about her all the time – I can't help but notice how her arrival, like yours, seemed like a miracle. But while she gifted us so much hope and joy and laughter, the truth is that these beautiful feelings were always inside of us, we had just lost sight of them behind the fear and anger and heartache that consumed us. So I ask each of you to choose your friends carefully, and to seek out the 'Penguins' in your life that can awaken the best aspects of your nature. And, most of all, I encourage you to be a 'Penguin' for others.

I hate my wheelchair and all that it represents, but there is still so much in this life that I love and am deeply grateful for. I love your father, our little home, the forest and ocean at our doorstep, and the endless blue sky. I love the sound of Australian songbirds – especially the magpies, obviously – and the warm golden light of a summer afternoon when we all sit outside on the front lawn.

But most of all I am so incredibly grateful that I didn't die so that now I get to watch my three boys grow up.

You are the best of everything this world has to offer, you are all my dreams come true at once, and I love you with all my heart.

Acknowledgments

This book is a testament to love and courage. Sharing any account of pain and suffering is difficult, and to draw something rich and beautiful from raw emotion and bitter heartache required the unwavering support of trusted colleagues, close friends and, above all, family.

Sam would like to thank her surfing sponsors: Blackmores, Hurley, LSD Surfboards, Deus Ex Machina, FCS, Quiksilver and Roxy, who make it possible for her to compete around the world.

Sam, Cam and BTG would like to acknowledge their two great publishing champions: Brigitta Doyle of HarperCollins Publishers, Australia, and Britta Egetemeier of Knaus Verlag, Germany.

They would also like to express their enduring gratitude to Sir Albert Zuckerman of Writers House, New York, and Jeanne Ryckmans of The Cameron Cresswell Agency, Sydney, for their guidance and encouragement.

And they would especially like to thank all the family, friends and supporters who have helped them raise funds and awareness for leading spinal cord injury charities around the world. Sam, Cam and BTG are each donating ten per cent of their royalties from the sale of this book to SpinalCure Australia (www.spinalcure.org.au) and they invite you to join them in supporting this life-changing charity in any way you can.

Not tomorrow.

Today.